CONTENTS

POEMS OF THOMAS CAREW (1595?–1639)

POEMS OF RICHARD CRASHAW (1612?–1649)

POEMS OF HENRY VAUGHAN (1621–1695)

EIGHT METAPHYSICAL POETS

*Edited with an Introduction
and Notes*

by

JACK DALGLISH

Heinemann Educational Publishers
Halley Court, Jordan Hill, Oxford OX2 8EJ
a division of Reed Educational & Professional Publishing Ltd

OXFORD MELBOURNE AUCKLAND
JOHANNESBURG BLANTYRE GABORONE
IBADAN PORTSMOUTH (NH) USA CHICAGO

ISBN 0 435 15031 6

INTRODUCTION AND NOTES
© JACK DALGLISH 1961
FIRST PUBLISHED 1961

01 02 03 28 27 26 25

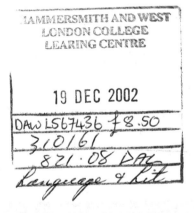
Printed in England by Clays Ltd, St Ives plc

INTRODUCTION

AN INDIVIDUAL account of each poet represented in this selection
will be found with the notes at the end of the volume. The purpose
of this introduction is to describe the *general* characteristics of
Metaphysical poetry. It must be realized that there are considerable
differences between the eight poets with whom we are concerned:
differences in talent, and differences in the extent to which the
various characteristics about to be described appear in the work
of each.

The poets whom we describe as 'The Metaphysicals' are those
who wrote during the seventeenth century under the influence of
John Donne, the first and greatest of them. We must remember
that Donne started to write about 1592, and Marvell died in 1678;
so that what we describe as 'Metaphysical Poetry' involves a
considerable period of time and great social, cultural and intellectual changes, as well as a number of individual personalities and
talents.

First, we may ask, why are these poets called 'Metaphysical'?
The term derives from a comment of Dryden's, and it has stuck;
but it is misleading. A metaphysical poet in the true sense would
be one whose work expressed a systematized and coherent philosophical or theological view of the nature of things: a poet such as
Lucretius, Dante or Milton. The Metaphysical poets were not of
this sort. Indeed, their work is often concerned with the lack of
coherence and certainty in the world in which they found themselves. Donne, for example, writes in *The first Anniversary*:

> And new Philosophy calls all in doubt,
> The Element of fire is quite put out;
> The Sun is lost, and th'earth, and no mans wit
> Can well direct him where to looke for it.

> And freely men confesse that this world's spent,
> When in the Planets, and the Firmament
> They seek so many new; they see that this
> Is crumbled out againe to his Atomies.
> 'Tis all in peeces, all cohaerence gone . . .

In this quotation, Donne is referring to the impact on traditional values and ways of thought of the implications of recent scientific and geographical discoveries. Such a preoccupation is typical of the intellectual atmosphere of England under the early Stuarts (Donne started writing in the 1590's, but was in many ways ahead of his time). The spirit of the time was very different from that of Elizabeth's heyday. Religious and political tensions already present during the last decade of Elizabeth's reign were exacerbated by the accession of her successor and grew in intensity until the explosion of the Civil War. The attitudes of modern empirical science began to replace those of mediaeval scholasticism and theology—for example, the theories of Copernicus, verified by Galileo's observations, were increasingly accepted, together with their implications, as the seventeenth century wore on. (The Royal Society received its charter in 1662, having originated in the Philosophical Society, founded in 1645). So the early seventeenth century was a time of political insecurity, religious controversy, and intellectual ferment; optimism and confidence had given way to a mood of questioning, of uncertainty, of scepticism, even of pessimism.

This is reflected in Metaphysical poetry. The typical Elizabethan poet had expressed comparatively simple and usually conventional themes in a style of conscious artifice and verbal elaboration. He produced mellifluous madrigals, charming love lyrics. The Metaphysical poets were far more intellectual, and their intellectuality is expressed in the matter and the manner of their poetry. They were intelligent, cultivated and often learned men; men, moreover, of affairs and wide experience, engaged in careers in the Church, in politics, at Court, or in the academic world. In their verse they sought to express and to explore ideas and feelings about the complex and changing world in which they lived, and also about their own natures; for new ideas about the nature of things had naturally been accompanied by a fresh interest in the psychology of the individual. Their learning and intellectual training were incorporated also in their mode of expression: they drew on their intellectual knowledge for much of the imagery by which their ideas and feelings were communicated, and they constantly analysed and argued about those ideas and feelings.

If the term 'Metaphysical' has any aptness at all to these poets, then, it is because it draws attention to the intellectual nature of their interests and attitudes and of their style. They were interested in their own experiences and in the movement of thought and attitudes in the world about them, and their interest was of an analytical nature. Their poems develop along the lines of logical argument; the poet examines a feeling, explores its ramifications, and seeks to throw new light on it by viewing it from new and unexpected angles and by finding connections between it and his intellectual concepts. Moreover, intellectual concepts themselves generated feeling in these poets; as Mr. T. S. Eliot has said: 'A thought to Donne was an experience: it modified his sensibility.'[1] So it is that in Metaphysical poetry we find a remarkable fusion of thought and feeling; whereas in Augustan poetry the intellect is predominant, and in nineteenth-century poetry the ideal is 'poetry conceived and composed in the soul' (Matthew Arnold). This is not to say that Augustan poets did not feel and Romantic poets did not think; but their feeling and thinking did not harmonize and interact, as did that of the Metaphysicals, so that (to quote Mr. Eliot again) 'the intellect was at the tip of the senses'.[2]

This fusion of thought and feeling is clearly seen when we consider Metaphysical imagery. All imagery is based upon the perception of some similarity between different things; but the

---

[1] 'The Metaphysical Poets' in *Selected Essays*, Faber & Faber.
[2] Ibid.

comparisons that a Metaphysical poet will make to communicate an idea are often startling to a reader conditioned by, say, Victorian poetry. A famous example is Donne's comparison, in *A Valediction forbidding mourning*, of two lovers to a pair of compasses:

> If they be two, they are two so
> As stiffe twin compasses are two,
> Thy soul, the fixt foot, makes no show
> To move, but doth, if th'other doe.

In fact, the characteristic that has often caused Metaphysical poetry to be described as 'fantastic' is the willingness of such a poet to illustrate, say, his relations with his mistress by reference to such intellectual interests as Ptolemaic astronomy, mathematics, or the recording of new geographical discoveries. It is important to realize, however, that this tendency is simply a sometimes bizarre result of the fact that the Metaphysical poet treats the whole of experience as poetic raw material. He is not confined for his sources of imagery to some such conception of 'the polite' or 'the poetical' as that which led Samuel Johnson to condemn Shakespeare's image of 'the blanket of the dark', or Tennyson to refer to the blood, sweat and grime on King Arthur's armour as 'drops of onset'. Donne may use an esoteric image such as that, in *A Nocturnall upon S. Lucies day*, of Love, as an alchemist, expressing 'a quintessence even from nothingnesse', which we cannot understand unless we realize that 'quintessence' here means the purest essence obtainable by distillation; but he also uses images of such a mundane nature as that of repairing a building, in the first two lines of one of his *Holy Sonnets*:

> Thou hast made me, And shall thy worke decay?
> Repaire me now . . .

and Vaughan, in a religious poem, introduces the image of a drunken man:

> But (ah!) my soul, with too much stay
> Is drunk, and staggers in the way . . .

4

A very important aspect of Metaphysical imagery is that it is used, not as mere ornament or illustration, but as a means of communicating thoughts and of exploring experience and achieving new insight into it. This is the purpose of the Metaphysical conceit. A conceit is an extended comparison, and the use of it is common in Elizabethan poetry. A famous example occurs in Shakespeare's *Richard II*, v, 5, when Richard compares at length his dungeon to a world, of which his thoughts are the inhabitants. In this example, however, and in most examples in Elizabethan poetry, the function of the conceit is largely ornamental. It is a set-piece, to be admired for its ingenuity. In Metaphysical poetry, however, the conceit is used as a means of exploring the experience it conveys; the development of the conceit is the development of the thought. Donne's image of the compasses, already mentioned, is an example of this; and there are longer ones, such as the conceit of the eclipse beginning in line 29 of King's *Exequy*. Moreover, whether developed into conceits or not, the images of these poets often have by their very unexpectedness the effect of jolting the reader into a new awareness of what the poet is trying to communicate, as with the unexpected image in the third line of this stanza of Herbert's:

> Only a sweet and virtuous soul
> Like season'd timber never gives;
> But though the whole world turn to coal,
> Then chiefly lives.

Metaphysical imagery is one of the instruments of minds of great flexibility and subtlety; and these qualities are shown also in the complexity of attitudes often to be found in Metaphysical poetry. If we examine a typical Victorian poem, we are likely to find that it is the direct expression of a simple emotion, and that it demands of the reader a solemn and straightforward response. In a Metaphysical poem, however serious the basic theme, we find not only a blend of passion and thought but an awareness of a variety of attitudes towards experience—an awareness which

5

expresses itself in what is called Metaphysical wit. It is this quality that enables Marvell, in *To his Coy Mistress*, to move from the extravagant humour of:

>   . . . I would
> Love you ten years before the Flood:
> And you should if you please refuse
> Till the Conversion of the *Jews*.
> My vegetable Love should grow
> Vaster than Empires, and more slow. . . .

to the haunting profundity of:

> But at my back I alwaies hear
> Times winged Charriot hurrying near:
> And yonder all before us lye
> Desarts of vast Eternity. . . .

and to express the main theme of the poem as a sort of grim joke:

> The Grave's a fine and private place,
> But none I think do there embrace.

It is this awareness also that occasions in these poets the use of puns in a perfectly serious context, to achieve not humour but a deeper realization of experience: thus Donne, in *A Hymne to God the Father*, puns on his own name:

> When thou hast done, thou hast not done,

and King, lamenting his dead wife, writes:

> And twixt me and my soules dear wish
> The earth now interposed is . . .

'the earth' representing both the planet causing the eclipse of his 'cleer Sun', as he calls his wife, and the soil with which her grave is filled.

I said earlier that Metaphysical imagery is not limited by

concepts of 'the poetical'. In the same way, there is no taint of 'poetic diction' in the words these poets use. Their language is that of refined, educated gentlemen of the world: direct, often colloquial, natural, idiomatic and quite free of any such conventional limitations as characterize Augustan or Victorian poetry. Consider the vivid naturalness of Herbert's:

> I struck the board, and cry'd, No more.
> I will abroad.
> What? shall I ever sigh and pine?

This quotation leads us to another aspect, or rather two related aspects, of Metaphysical poetry: its verse movement and the dramatic' quality to which this and its natural diction give rise. There have been times when critics, their ears attuned to poetry that is 'regular' or 'correct' in movement and avowedly separate from speech, have criticized Donne and his followers for 'harsh ruggedness' of rhythm. In fact, however, the characteristic Metaphysical handling of verse movement reproduces the natural stresses and intonations of the speaking voice and plays them against the exigencies of whatever verse form is being used. In *The Sunne Rising*, Donne employs a complicated and difficult stanza form, but he uses its rhymes and varying line lengths to obtain a remarkably natural effect:

> Busie old fool, unruly Sunne,
> Why dost thou thus,
> Through windowes, and through curtaines call on us?
> Must to thy motions lovers seasons run?
> Saucy pedantique wretch, goe chide
> Late schoole boys, and sowre prentices . . .

Observe the humorous vitality of the opening apostrophe, the naturalness of the tone of mock-indignant questioning, the extra emphasis which falls aptly on the rhyme word 'us', the contemptuous stress on 'thy', and the natural pause after the fourth

7

line, which precedes the change to scornful imperative. Henry King, in these lines from *The Exequy*, is using octosyllabic couplets:

> Mean time, thou hast her, earth: much good
> May my harm do thee. Since it stood
> With Heavens will I might not call
> Her longer mine, I give thee all
> My short-liv'd right and interest
> In her, whom living I lov'd best . . .

but the speech quality is such that one is reminded of dramatic blank verse. In fact, the characteristic movement of Metaphysical verse may fairly be described as dramatic, for the stress patterns are dictated by the meaning and the tone and seek to represent the movement of impassioned thought spoken aloud. As Dr. F. R. Leavis has pointed out, Donne's handling of the heroic couplet in *Satyre iii* has affinities with Shakespeare's mature blank verse, though it is in fact something quite different:

> Are not heavens joyes as valiant to asswage
> Lusts, as earths honour was to them? Alas,
> As wee do them in meanes, shall they surpasse
> Us in the end, and shall thy fathers spirit
> Meete blinde Philosophers in heaven, whose merit
> Of strict life may be imputed faith, and heare
> Thee, whom hee taught so easie wayes and neare
> To follow, damn'd?

Yet the same poet can produce the lyrical grace of *Sweetest love, I do not go*.

I have said that the Metaphysical poets were followers of Donne, and this is true; but there was another potent influence on their work—Donne's friend and contemporary, Ben Jonson. Jonson's poetry differs greatly from Donne's. It is a poetry of statement, without the 'undergrowth' of evocation through associations that Donne's use of imagery produces, and without the argumentative subtleties of Donne's method. But Jonson had modelled himself on classical authors, and was able to reproduce in English poetry

8

their poise and grace, assimilated into English idiom. It is this conscious poise, this elegant urbanity of tone, movement and attitude, that we find reflected in much of the poetry of Donne's successors, notably in that of Carew and Marvell. The combination of Donne's influence with Jonson's is apparent in these lines of Marvell's (but do not let us forget that it is Marvell's peculiar genius that is able to combine them with such effect):

> As Lines so Loves *oblique* may well
> Themselves in every Angle greet:
> But ours so truly *Parallel*,
> Though infinite can never meet.
>
> Therefore the Love which us doth bind,
> But Fate so enviously debars,
> Is the Conjunction of the Mind,
> And Opposition of the Stars.

In these stanzas, the sources of the imagery and the way in which it is used to explore the experience and communicate the thought derive from Donne; but the elegant balance of the verse movement and the sense of sophisticated poise have an evident relation to such stanzas of Jonson's as:

> Though beauty be the mark of praise,
>   And yours of whom I sing be such
> As not the world can praise too much,
>   Yet 'tis your Virtue now I raise:
>
> A virtue, like allay so gone
>   Throughout your form as, though that move
> And draw and conquer all men's love,
>   This subjects you to love of one.

The Metaphysical poet, then, is characteristically intellectual and introspective. His poems develop by the process of logical argument, and his imagery ranges over an unlimited field of experience, intellectual and otherwise. He is sensitive to and interested in the

9

complexities and subtleties of experience; and his sensitivity expresses itself in flexibility of attitude and tone. His diction is free from convention, and he is acutely aware of the resources of words, so that he packs meaning into them and frequently uses puns. His handling of verse is remarkably skilful and sure, and he combines an ability to suggest the idiom and movement of speech with the successful handling of difficult stanza forms. Above all, he demands complete concentration and an agile emotional, intellectual and sensory response from the reader.

Metaphysical poetry has been called obscure and difficult. It will usually be found, however, that, apart from the relatively few occasions (likely to occur in the literature of any period) when specialized knowledge of some contemporary interest or circumstance is necessary, concentration on the reader's part will bring enlightenment and a satisfaction all the greater for the effort required. For all art demands an effort of response; and the less it demands, the less it is likely to give of lasting value.

ACKNOWLEDGEMENT

FOR THE text of the poems and for the elucidation of many difficulties I am indebted to the Oxford standard editions and to Mr. J. Sparrow's edition of *Poems of Henry King* (Nonesuch Press).

JOHN DONNE

The Good-morrow

I wonder by my troth, what thou, and I
Did, till we lov'd? were we not wean'd till then?
But suck'd on countrey pleasures, childishly?
Or snorted we in the seaven sleepers den?
T'was so; But this, all pleasures fancies bee.   5
If ever any beauty I did see,
Which I desir'd, and got, t'was but a dreame of thee.

And now good morrow to our waking soules,
Which watch not one another out of feare;
For love, all love of other sights controules,   10
And makes one little roome, an every where.
Let sea-discoverers to new worlds have gone,
Let Maps to others, worlds on worlds have showne,
Let us possesse one world, each hath one, and is one.

My face in thine eye, thine in mine appeares,   15
And true plaine hearts doe in the faces rest,
Where can we finde two better hemispheares
Without sharpe North, without declining West?
What ever dies, was not mixt equally;
If our two loves be one, or, thou and I   20
Love so alike, that none doe slacken, none can die.

The Sunne Rising

Busie old foole, unruly Sunne,
Why dost thou thus,
Through windowes, and through curtaines call on us?
Must to thy motions lovers seasons run?
Sawcy pedantique wretch, goe chide   5
Late schoole boyes, and sowre prentices,
Goe tell Court-huntsmen, that the King will ride,
Call countrey ants to harvest offices;
Love, all alike, no season knowes, nor clyme,
Nor houres, dayes, moneths, which are the rags of time.   10

Thy beames, so reverend, and strong
Why shouldst thou thinke?
I could eclipse and cloud them with a winke,
But that I would not lose her sight so long:
If her eyes have not blinded thine,   15
Looke, and to morrow late, tell mee,
Whether both the'India's of spice and Myne
Be where thou leftst them, or lie here with mee.
Aske for those Kings whom thou saw'st yesterday,
And thou shalt heare, All here in one bed lay.   20

She'is all States, and all Princes, I,
Nothing else is.
Princes doe but play us; compar'd to this,
All honor's mimique; All wealth alchimie,
Thou sunne art halfe as happy'as wee,   25
In that the world's contracted thus;

Thine age askes ease, and since thy duties bee
  To warme the world, that's done in warming us.
Shine here to us, and thou art every where;
This bed thy centre is, these walls, thy spheare.   30

Song

Sweetest love, I do not goe,
  For wearinesse of thee,
Nor in hope the world can show
  A fitter Love for mee;
    But since that I   5
Must dye at last, 'tis best,
To use my selfe in jest
  Thus by fain'd deaths to dye;

Yesternight the Sunne went hence,
  And yet is here to day,   10
He hath no desire nor sense,
  Nor halfe so short a way:
    Then feare not mee,
But beleeve that I shall make
Speedier journeys, since I take   15
  More wings and spurres than hee.

O how feeble is mans power,
  That if good fortune fall,
Cannot adde another houre,
  Nor a lost houre recall!   20
    But come bad chance,

And wee joyne to'it our strength,
And wee teach it art and length,
  It selfe o'er us to'advance.

When thou sigh'st, thou sigh'st not winde,   25
  But sigh'st my soule away,
When thou weep'st, unkindly kinde,
  My lifes blood doth decay.
    It cannot bee
That thou lov'st mee, as thou say'st,   30
If in thine my life thou waste,
  Thou art the best of mee.

Let not thy divining heart
  Forethinke me any ill,
Destiny may take thy part,   35
  And may thy feares fulfill;
    But thinke that wee
Are but turn'd aside to sleepe;
They who one another keepe
  Alive, ne'er parted bee.   40

The Anniversarie

All Kings, and all their favorites,
  All glory of honors, beauties, wits,
The Sun it selfe, which makes times, as they passe,
Is elder by a yeare, now, than it was
When thou and I first one another saw: 5
All other things, to their destruction draw,
  Only our love hath no decay;
This, no to morrow hath, nor yesterday,

Running it never runs from us away,
But truly keepes his first, last, everlasting day.   10

   Two graves must hide thine and my corse,
    If one might, death were no divorce.
Alas, as well as other Princes, wee,
(Who Prince enough in one another bee,)
Must leave at last in death, these eyes, and eares,   15
Oft fed with true oathes, and with sweet salt teares;
   But soules where nothing dwells but love
(All other thoughts being inmates) then shall prove
This, or a love increased there above,
When bodies to their graves, soules from their graves remove. 20

   And then wee shall be throughly blest,
    But wee no more, than all the rest;
Here upon earth, we'are Kings, and none but wee
Can be such Kings, nor of such subjects bee.
Who is so safe as wee? where none can doe   25
Treason to us, except one of us two.
   True and false feares let us refraine,
Let us love nobly, and live, and adde againe
Yeares and yeares unto yeares, till we attaine
To write threescore: this is the second of our raigne.   30

Twicknam garden

   Blasted with sighs, and surrounded with teares,
    Hither I come to seeke the spring,
    And at mine eyes, and at mine eares,
   Receive such balmes, as else cure every thing;

But O, selfe traytor, I do bring   5
The spider love, which transubstantiates all,
    And can convert Manna to gall,
And that this place may thoroughly be thought
    True Paradise, I have the serpent brought.

'Twere wholsomer for mee, that winter did   10
    Benight the glory of this place,
    And that a grave frost did forbid
These trees to laugh, and mocke mee to my face;
    But that I may not this disgrace
Indure, nor yet leave loving, Love let mee   15
    Some senslesse peece of this place bee;
Make me a mandrake, so I may groane here,
    Or a stone fountaine weeping out my yeare.

Hither with christall vyals, lovers come,
    And take my teares, which are loves wine,   20
    And try your mistresse Teares at home,
For all are false, that taste not just like mine;
    Alas, hearts do not in eyes shine,
Nor can you more judge womans thoughts by teares,
    Than by her shadow, what she weares.   25
O perverse sexe, where none is true but shee,
    Who's therefore true, because her truth kills mee.

A Valediction: of weeping

    Let me powre forth
    My teares before thy face, whil'st I stay here,
For thy face coines them, and thy stampe they beare,
And by this Mintage they are something worth,

For thus they bee 5
Pregnant of thee;
Fruits of much griefe they are, emblems of more,
When a teare falls, that thou falst which it bore,
So thou and I are nothing then, when on a diverse shore.

On a round ball 10
A workeman that hath copies by, can lay
An Europe, Afrique, and an Asia,
And quickly make that, which was nothing, *All*,
So doth each teare,
Which thee doth weare, 15
A globe, yea world by that impression grow,
Till thy teares mixt with mine doe overflow
This world, by waters sent from thee, my heaven dissolved so.

O more than Moone,
Draw not up seas to drowne me in thy spheare, 20
Weepe me not dead, in thine armes, but forbeare
To teach the sea, what it may doe too soone;
Let not the winde
Example finde,
To doe me more harme, than it purposeth; 25
Since thou and I sigh one anothers breath,
Who e'er sighes most, is cruellest, and hastes the others death.

A nocturnall upon S. Lucies day,

Being the shortest day

Tis the yeares midnight, and it is the dayes,
Lucies, who scarce seaven houres herself unmaskes,
The Sunne is spent, and now his flasks
Send forth light squibs, no constant rayes;

The worlds whole sap is sunke: 5
The generall balme th'hydroptique earth hath drunk,
Whither, as to the beds-feet, life is shrunke,
Dead and enterr'd; yet all these seeme to laugh,
Compar'd with me, who am their Epitaph.

Study me then, you who shall lovers bee 10
At the next world, that is, at the next Spring:
    For I am every dead thing,
    In whom love wrought new Alchimie.
        For his art did expresse
A quintessence even from nothingnesse, 15
From dull privations, and leane emptinesse:
He ruin'd mee, and I am re-begot
Of absence, darknesse, death; things which are not.

All others, from all things, draw all that's good,
Life, soule, forme, spirit, whence they beeing have; 20
    I, by loves limbecke, am the grave
    Of all, that's nothing. Oft a flood
        Have wee two wept, and so
Drownd the whole world, us two; oft did we grow
To be two Chaosses, when we did show 25
Care to ought else; and often absences
Withdrew our soules, and made us carcasses.

But I am by her death, (which word wrongs her)
Of the first nothing, the Elixer grown;
    Were I a man, that I were one, 30
    I needs must know; I should preferre,
        If I were any beast,
Some ends, some means; Yea plants, yea stones detest,
And love; All, all some properties invest;
If I an ordinary nothing were, 35
As shadow, a light, and body must be here.

18

But I am None; nor will my Sunne renew.
You lovers, for whose sake, the lesser Sunne
    At this time to the Goat is runne
    To fetch new lust, and give it you,   40
        Enjoy your summer all;
Since shee enjoyes her long nights festivall,
Let mee prepare towards her, and let mee call
This houre her Vigill, and her Eve, since this
Both the yeares, and the dayes deep midnight is.   45

A Valediction: forbidding mourning

As virtuous men passe mildly away,
    And whisper to their soules, to goe,
Whilst some of their sad friends doe say,
    The breath goes now, and some say, no:

So let us melt, and make no noise,   5
    No teare-floods, nor sigh-tempests move,
T'were prophanation of our joyes
    To tell the layetie our love.

Moving of th'earth brings harmes and feares,
    Men reckon what it did and meant,   10
But trepidation of the spheares,
    Though greater farre, is innocent.

    Dull sublunary lovers love
    (Whose soule is sense) cannot admit
Absence, because it doth remove   15
    Those things which elemented it.

But we by a love, so much refin'd,
   That our selves know not what it is,
Inter-assured of the mind,
   Care lesse, eyes, lips, and hands to misse.   20

Our two soules therefore, which are one,
   Though I must goe, endure not yet
A breach, but an expansion,
   Like gold to aiery thinnesse beate.

If they be two, they are two so   25
   As stiffe twin compasses are two,
Thy soule the fixt foot, makes no show
   To move, but doth, if the'other doe.

And though it in the center sit,
   Yet when the other far doth rome,   30
It leanes, and hearkens after it,
   And growes erect, as that comes home.

Such wilt thou be to mee, who must
   Like th'other foot, obliquely runne;
Thy firmness makes my circle just,   35
   And makes me end, where I begunne.

The Extasie

Where, like a pillow on a bed,
   A Pregnant banke swel'd up, to rest
The violets reclining head,
   Sat we two, one anothers best.

Our hands were firmely cimented   5
   With a fast balme, which thence did spring,
Our eye-beames twisted, and did thred
   Our eyes, upon one double string;
So to'entergraft our hands, as yet
   Was all the meanes to make us one,   10
And pictures in our eyes to get
   Was all our propagation.
As 'twixt two equal Armies, Fate
   Suspends uncertaine victorie,
Our soules, (which to advance their state,   15
   Were gone out,) hung 'twixt her, and mee.
And whil'st our soules negotiate there,
   Wee like sepulchrall statues lay;
All day, the same our postures were,
   And wee said nothing, all the day.   20
If any, so by love refin'd,
   That he soules language understood,
And by good love were growen all minde,
   Within convenient distance stood,
He (though he knew not which soul spake,   25
   Because both meant, both spake the same)
Might thence a new concoction take,
   And part farre purer than he came.
This Extasie doth unperplex
   (We said) and tell us what we love,   30
Wee see by this, it was not sexe,
   Wee see, we saw not what did move:
But as all severall soules containe
   Mixture of things, they know not what,
Love, these mixt soules, doth mixe againe,   35
   And makes both one, each this and that.
A single violet transplant,
   The strength, the colour, and the size,

(All which before was poore, and scant,)
  Redoubles still, and multiplies.   40
When love, with one another so
  Interinanimates two soules,
That abler soule, which thence doth flow,
  Defects of lonelinesse controules.
Wee then, who are this new soule, know,   45
  Of what we are compos'd, and made,
For, th'Atomies of which we grow,
  Are soules, whom no change can invade.
But O alas, so long, so farre
  Our bodies why doe wee forbeare?   50
They'are ours, though they'are not wee, Wee are
  The intelligences, they the spheare.
We owe them thankes, because they thus,
  Did us, to us, at first convay,
Yeelded their forces, sense, to us,   55
  Nor are drosse to us, but allay.
On man heavens influence workes not so,
  But that it first imprints the ayre,
Soe soule into the soule may flow,
  Though it to body first repaire.   60
As our blood labours to beget
  Spirits, as like soules as it can,
Because such fingers need to knit
  That subtile knot, which makes us man:
So must pure lovers soules descend   65
  T'affections, and to faculties,
Which sense may reach and apprehend,
  Else a great Prince in prison lies.
To'our bodies turne wee then, that so
  Weake men on love reveal'd may looke   70
Loves mysteries in soules doe grow,
  But yet the body is his booke.

And if some lover, such as wee,
    Have heard this dialogue of one,
Let him still marke us, he shall see   75
    Small change, when we'are to bodies gone.

The Funerall

Who ever comes to shroud me, do not harme
    Nor question much
That subtile wreath of haire, which crowns my arme;
The mystery, the signe you must not touch,
    For 'tis my outward Soule,   5
Viceroy to that, which then to heaven being gone,
    Will leave this to controule,
And keepe these limbes, her Provinces, from dissolution.

For if the sinewie thread my braine lets fall
    Through every part,   10
Can tye those parts, and make mee one of all;
These haires which upward grew, and strength and art
    Have from a better braine,
Can better do'it; Except she meant that I
    By this should know my pain,   15
As prisoners then are manacled, when they'are condemn'd to die.

What e'er shee meant by'it, bury it with me,
    For since I am
Loves martyr, it might breed idolatrie,
If into other hands these Reliques came;   20
    As 'twas humility
To afford to it all that a Soule can doe,
    So, 'tis some bravery,
That since you would save none of mee, I bury some of you.

Elegie v. His Picture

Here take my Picture; though I bid farewell,
Thine, in my heart, where my soule dwells, shall dwell.
'Tis like me now, but I dead, 'twill be more
When wee are shadowes both, than 'twas before.
When weather-beaten I come backe; my hand,   5
Perhaps with rude oares torne, or Sun-beams tann'd,
My face and brest of haircloth, and my head
With cares rash sodaine hoarinesse o'erspread,
My body'a sack of bones, broken within,
And powders blew staines scatter'd on my skinne;   10
If rivall fooles taxe thee to'have lov'd a man,
So foule, and coarse, as, Oh, I may seeme than,
This shall say what I was: and thou shalt say,
Doe his hurts reach mee? doth my worth decay?
Or doe they reach his judging minde, that hee   15
Should now love lesse, what hee did love to see?
That which in him was faire and delicate,
Was but the milke, which in loves childish state
Did nurse it: who now'is growne strong enough
To feed on that, which to disused tastes seemes tough.   20

Satyre iii

Kinde pitty chokes my spleene; brave scorn forbids
Those teares to issue which swell my eye-lids;
I must not laugh, nor weepe sinnes, and be wise,
Can railing then cure these worne maladies?

Is not our Mistresse faire Religion, 5
As worthy of all our Soules devotion,
As vertue was to the first blinded age?
Are not heavens joyes as valiant to asswage
Lusts, as earths honour was to them? Alas,
As wee do them in meanes, shall they surpasse 10
Us in the end, and shall thy fathers spirit
Meete blinde Philosophers in heaven, whose merit
Of strict life may be imputed faith, and heare
Thee, whom hee taught so easie wayes and neare
To follow, damn'd? O if thou dar'st, feare this; 15
This feare great courage, and high valour is.
Dar'st thou ayd mutinous Dutch, and dar'st thou lay
Thee in ships woodden Sepulchers, a prey
To leaders rage, to stormes, to shot, to dearth?
Dar'st thou dive seas, and dungeons of the earth? 20
Hast thou couragious fire to thaw the ice
Of frozen North discoueries? and thrice
Colder than Salamanders, like divine
Children in th'oven, fires of Spaine, and the line,
Whose countries limbecks to our bodies bee, 25
Canst thou for gaine beare? and must every hee
Which cryes not, Goddesse, to thy Mistresse, draw,
Or eate thy poysonous words? courage of straw!
O desperate coward, wilt thou seeme bold, and
To thy foes and his (who made thee to stand 30
Sentinell in his worlds garrison) thus yeeld,
And for forbidden warres, leave th'appointed field?
Know thy foes: The foule Devill (whom thou
Strivest to please,) for hate, not love, would allow
Thee faine, his whole Realme to be quit; and as 35
The worlds all parts wither away and passe,
So the worlds selfe, thy other lov'd foe, is
In her decrepit wayne, and thou loving this,

Dost love a withered and worne strumpet; last,
Flesh (it selfes death) and joyes which flesh can taste, 40
Thou lovest; and thy faire goodly soule, which doth
Give this flesh power to taste joy, thou dost loath.
Seeke true religion. O where? Mirreus
Thinking her unhous'd here, and fled from us,
Seekes her at Rome; there, because hee doth know 45
That shee was there a thousand yeares agoe,
He loves her ragges so, as wee here obey
The statecloth where the Prince sate yesterday.
Crantz to such brave Loves will not be inthrall'd,
But loves her onely, who at Geneva is call'd 50
Religion, plaine, simple, sullen, yong,
Contemptuous, yet unhansome; As among
Lecherous humors, there is one that judges
No wenches wholsome, but course country drudges.
Graius stayes still at home here, and because 55
Some Preachers, vile ambitious bauds, and lawes
Still new like fashions, bid him thinke that shee
Which dwells with us, is onely perfect, hee
Imbraceth her, whom his Godfathers will
Tender to him, being tender, as Wards still 60
Take such wives as their Guardians offer, or
Pay valewes. Carelesse Phrygius doth abhorre
All, because all cannot be good, as one
Knowing some women whores, dares marry none.
Gracchus loves all as one, and thinkes that so 65
As women do in divers countries goe
In divers habits, yet are still one kinde,
So doth, so is Religion; and this blind-
nesse too much light breeds; but unmoved thou
Of force must one, and forc'd but one allow; 70
And the right; aske thy father which is shee,
Let him aske his; though truth and falshood bee

Iveare twins, yet truth a little elder is;
Be busie to seeke her, beleeve mee this,
Hee's not of none, nor worst, that seekes the best.   75
To adore, or scorne an image, or protest,
May all be bad; doubt wisely; in strange way
To stand inquiring right, is not to stray;
To sleepe, or runne wrong, is. On a huge hill,
Cragged, and steep, Truth stands, and hee that will   80
Reach her, about must, and about must goe;
And what the hills suddennes resists, winne so;
Yet strive so, that before age, deaths twilight,
Thy Soule rest, for none can worke in that night.
To will, implyes delay, therefore now doe: 85
Hard deeds, the bodies paines; hard knowledge too
The mindes indeavours reach, and mysteries
Are like the Sunne, dazling, yet plaine to all eyes.
Keepe the truth which thou hast found; men do not stand
In so ill case here, that God hath with his hand   90
Sign'd Kings blank-charters to kill whom they hate,
Nor are they Vicars, but hangmen to Fate.
Foole and wretch, wilt thou let thy Soule be tyed
To mans lawes, by which she shall not be tryed
At the last day? Oh, will it then boot thee   95
To say a Philip, or a Gregory,
A Harry, or a Martin taught thee this?
Is not this excuse for mere contraries,
Equally strong? cannot both sides say so?
That thou mayest rightly obey power, her bounds know;   100
Those past, her nature, and name is chang'd; to be
Then humble to her is idolatrie.
As streames are, Power is; those blest flowers that dwell
At the rough streames calme head, thrive and do well,
But having left their roots, and themselves given   105
To the streames tyrannous rage, alas, are driven

Through mills, and rockes, and woods, and at last, almost
Consum'd in going, in the sea are lost:
So perish Soules, which more chuse mens unjust
Power from God claym'd, than God himselfe to trust.　　110

Holy Sonnets

i

Thou hast made me, and shall thy worke decay?
Repaire me now, for now mine end doth haste,
I runne to death, and death meets me as fast,
And all my pleasures are like yesterday;
I dare not move my dimme eyes any way,　　5
Despaire behind, and death before doth cast
Such terrour, and my feeble flesh doth waste
By sinne in it, which it t'wards hell doth weigh;
Only thou art above, and when towards thee
By thy leave I can looke, I rise againe;　　10
But our old subtle foe so tempteth me,
That not one houre my selfe I can sustaine;
Thy Grace may wing me to prevent his art,
And thou like Adamant draw mine iron heart.

vii

At the round earths imagin'd corners, blow
Your trumpets, Angells, and arise, arise
From death, you numberlesse infinities
Of soules, and to your scattred bodies goe,
All whom the flood did, and fire shall o'erthrow,　　5
All whom warre, dearth, age, agues, tyrannies,
Despaire, law, chance, hath slaine, and you whose eyes,
Shall behold God, and never taste deaths woe.

But let them sleepe, Lord, and mee mourne a space,
For, if above all these, my sinnes abound,   10
'Tis late to aske abundance of thy grace,
When wee are there; here on this lowly ground,
Teach mee how to repent; for that's as good
As if thou'hadst seal'd my pardon, with thy blood.

x

Death be not proud, though some have called thee
Mighty and dreadfull, for, thou art not soe,
For, those, whom thou think'st, thou dost overthrow,
Die not, poore death, nor yet canst thou kill mee.
From rest and sleepe, which but thy pictures bee,   5
Much pleasure, then from thee much more must flow,
And soonest our best men with thee doe goe,
Rest of their bones, and soules deliverie.
Thou art slave to Fate, Chance, kings, and desperate men,
And dost with poyson, warre, and sicknesse dwell,   10
And poppie, or charmes can make us sleepe as well,
And better than thy stroake; why swell'st thou then?
One short sleepe past, wee wake eternally,
And death shall be no more; death, thou shalt die.

xiv

Batter my heart, three person'd God; for, you
As yet but knocke, breathe, shine, and seeke to mend;
That I may rise, and stand, o'erthrow mee,'and bend
Your force, to breake, blowe, burn and make me new.
I, like an usurpt towne, to'another due,   5
Labour to'admit you, but Oh, to no end,
Reason your viceroy in mee, mee should defend,
But is captiv'd, and proves weake or untrue.
Yet dearely'I love you, and would be loved faine,

29

But am betroth'd unto your enemie: 10
Divorce mee, untie, or breake that knot againe,
Take mee to you, imprison mee, for I
Except you'enthrall mee, never shall be free,
Nor ever chaste, except you ravish mee.

Hymne to God my God, in my sicknesse

Since I am comming to that Holy roome,
　　Where, with thy Quire of Saints for evermore,
I shall be made thy Musique; As I come
　　I tune the Instrument here at the dore,
　　And what I must doe then, thinke here before.   5

Whilst my Physitians by their love are growne
　　Cosmographers, and I their Mapp, who lie
Flat on this bed, that by them may be showne
　　That this is my South-west discoverie
　　Per fretum febris, by these streights to die,   10

I joy, that in these straits, I see my West;
　　For, though theire currants yeeld returne to none,
What shall my West hurt me? As West and East
　　In all flatt Maps (and I am one) are one,
　　So death doth touch the Resurrection.   15

Is the Pacifique Sea my home? Or are
The Easterne riches? Is *Ierusalem*?
Anyan, and *Magellan*, and *Gibraltare*,
　　All streights, and none but streights, are wayes to them,
　　Whether where *Iaphet* dwelt, or *Cham*, or *Sem*.   20

We thinke that *Paradise* and *Calvarie*,
  Christs Crosse, and *Adams* tree, stood in one place;
Looke Lord, and finde both *Adams* met in me;
  As the first *Adams* sweat surrounds my face,
  May the last *Adams* blood my soule embrace.   25

So, in his purple wrapp'd receive mee Lord,
  By these his thornes give me his other Crowne;
And as to others soules I preach'd thy word,
  Be this my Text, my Sermon to mine owne,
  Therfore that he may raise the Lord throws down.   30

A Hymne to God the Father

Wilt thou forgive that sinne where I begunne,
  Which is my sin, though it were done before?
Wilt thou forgive those sinnes, through which I runne,
  And do run still: though still I do deplore?
    When thou hast done, thou hast not done,   5
      For, I have more.

Wilt thou forgive that sinne by which I'have wonne
  Others to sinne? and, made my sinne their doore?
Wilt thou forgive that sinne which I did shunne
  A yeare, or two: but wallowed in, a score?   10
    When thou hast done, thou hast not done,
      For I have more.

I have a sinne of feare, that when I have spunne
  My last thred, I shall perish on the shore;
Sweare by thy selfe, that at my death, thy sonne   15
  Shall shine as he shines now, and heretofore;
    And, having done that, Thou hast done,
      I feare no more.

GEORGE HERBERT

Affliction

When first thou didst entice to thee my heart,
      I thought the service brave:
So many joyes I writ down for my part,
      Besides what I might have
Out of my stock of naturall delights,   5
Augmented with thy gracious benefits.

I looked on thy furniture so fine,
      And made it fine to me:
Thy glorious household-stuffe did me entwine,
      And 'tice me unto thee;   10
Such starres I counted mine: both heav'n and earth
Payd me my wages in a world of mirth.

What pleasures could I want, whose King I served?
      Where joyes my fellows were.
Thus argu'd into hopes, my thoughts reserved   15
      No place for grief or fear.
Therefore my sudden soul caught at the place,
And made her youth and fiercenesse seek thy face.

At first thou gav'st me milk and sweetnesses;
      I had my wish and way: 20
My dayes were straw'd with flow'rs and happinesse;
      There was no month but May.
But with my yeares sorrow did twist and grow,
And made a partie unawares for wo.

My flesh began unto my soul in pain,   25
         Sicknesses cleave my bones;
Consuming agues dwell in ev'ry vein,
         And tune my breath to grones.
Sorrow was all my soul; I scarce beleeved,
Till grief did tell me roundly, that I lived.   30

When I got health, thou took'st away my life,
         And more; for my friends die:
My mirth and edge was lost; a blunted knife
         Was of more use than I.
Thus thinne and lean without a fence or friend,   35
I was blown through with ev'ry storm and winde.

Whereas my birth and spirit rather took
         The way that takes the town;
Thou didst betray me to a lingring book,
         And wrap me in a gown.   40
I was entangled in the world of strife,
Before I had the power to change my life.

Yet, for I threatned oft the siege to raise,
         Not simpring all mine age,
Thou often didst with Academick praise   45
         Melt and dissolve my rage.
I took thy sweetned pill, till I came where
I could not go away, nor persevere.

Yet lest perchance I should too happie be
         In my unhappinesse,   50
Turning my purge to food, thou throwest me
         Into more sicknesses.
Thus doth thy power crosse-bias me, not making
Thine own gift good, yet me from my wayes taking.

Now I am here, what thou wilt do with me 55
     None of my books will show:
I reade, and sigh, and wish I were a tree;
     For sure then I should grow
To fruit or shade: at least some bird would trust
Her household to me, and I should be just. 60

Yet, though thou troublest me, I must be meek;
     In weaknesse must be stout.
Well, I will change the service, and go seek
     Some other master out.
Ah my deare God! though I am clean forgot, 65
Let me not love thee, if I love thee not.

The Pearl

Matthew xiii 45

I know the wayes of Learning; both the head
And pipes that feed the presse, and make it runne;
What reason hath from nature borrowed,
Or of it self, like a good huswife spunne
In laws and policie; what the starres conspire, 5
What willing nature speaks, what forc'd by fire;
Both th'old discoveries, and the new-found seas,
The stock and surplus, cause and historie:
All these stand open, or I have the keys:
     Yet I love thee. 10

I know the wayes of Honour, what maintains
The quick returns of courtesie and wit:
In vies of favours whether partie gains,

When glorie swells the heart, and moldeth it
To all expressions both of hand and eye,   15
Which on the world a true-love-knot may tie.
And bear the bundle, wheresoe're it goes:
How many drammes of spirit there must be
To sell my life unto my friends or foes:
        Yet I love thee.   20

I know the wayes of Pleasure, the sweet strains,
The lullings and the relishes of it;
The propositions of hot bloud and brains;
What mirth and musick mean; what love and wit
Have done these twentie hundred yeares, and more: 25
I know the projects of unbridled store:
My stuffe is flesh, not brasse; my senses live,
And grumble oft, that they have more in me
Then he that curbs them, being but one to five:
        Yet I love thee.   30

I know all these, and have them in my hand:
Therefore not sealed, but with open eyes
I flie to thee, and fully understand
Both the main sale, and the commodities;
And at what rate and price I have thy love;   35
With all the circumstances that may move:
Yet through these labyrinths, not my groveling wit,
But thy silk twist let down from heav'n to me,
Did both conduct and teach me, how by it
        To climbe to thee.   40

Prayer

Prayer the Churches banquet, Angels age,
   Gods breath in man returning to his birth,
The soul in paraphrase, heart in pilgrimage,
   The Christian plummet sounding heav'n and earth;

Engine against th'Almightie, sinners towre,   5
   Reversed thunder, Christ-side-piercing spear,
The six-daies world transposing in an houre,
   A kinde of tune, which all things heare and fear;

Softnesse, and peace, and joy, and love, and blisse,
   Exalted Manna, gladnesse of the best,   10
   Heaven in ordinarie, man well drest,
The milkie way, the bird of Paradise,

   Church-bells beyond the starres heard, the souls blood,
   The land of spices, something understood.

Redemption

Having been tenant long to a rich Lord,
   Not thriving, I resolved to be bold,
   And make a suit unto him, to afford
A new small-rented lease, and cancell th' old.

In heaven at his manor I him sought: 5
    They told me there, that he was lately gone
    About some land, which he had dearly bought
Long since on earth, to take possession.

I straight return'd, and knowing his great birth,
    Sought him accordingly in great resorts;   10
    In cities, theatres, gardens, parks, and courts:
At length I heard a ragged noise and mirth

    Of theeves and murderers: there I him espied,
    Who straight, *Your suit is granted*, said, & died.

Easter

I got me flowers to straw thy way,
    I got me boughs off many a tree,
But thou wast up by break of day,
    And brought'st thy sweets along with thee.

The Sunne arising in the East,   5
    Though he give light, and th' East perfume,
If they should offer to contest
    With thy arising, they presume.

Can there be any day but this,
    Though many sunnes to shine endeavour?   10
We count three hundred, but we misse;
    There is but one, and that one ever.

Easter Wings

Lord, who createdst man in wealth and store,
  Though foolishly he lost the same,
    Decaying more and more,
      Till he became
        Most poore: 5
        With thee
        O let me rise
      As larks, harmoniously,
    And sing this day thy victories:
Then shall the fall further the flight in me.   10

My tender age in sorrow did beginne:
  And still with sicknesses and shame
    Thou didst so punish sinne,
      That I became
        Most thinne.   15
        With thee
        Let me combine,
      And feel this day thy victorie:
    For, if I imp my wing on thine,
Affliction shall advance the flight in me.   20

Jordan

Who sayes that fictions onely and false hair
Become a verse? Is there in truth no beautie?
Is all good structure in a winding stair?
May no lines passe, except they do their dutie
    Not to a true, but painted chair?   5

Is it no verse, except enchanted groves
And sudden arbours shadow course-spunne lines?
Must purling streams refresh a lovers loves?
Must all be vail'd, while he that reades, divines,
    Catching the sense at two removes?   10

Shepherds are honest people; let them sing:
Riddle who list, for me, and pull for Prime:
I envie no mans nightingale or spring;
Nor let them punish me with losse of ryme,
    Who plainly say, *My God, My King*.   15

The Church Windows

Lord, how can man preach thy eternall word?
    He is a brittle crazie glasse:
Yet in thy temple thou dost him afford
    This glorious and transcendent place,
    To be a window, through thy grace.   5

But when thou dost anneal in glasse thy storie,
    Making thy life to shine within
The holy Preachers; then the light and glorie
    More rev'rend grows, & more doth win;
    Which else shows watrish, bleak, & thin.   10

Doctrine and life, colours and light, in one
    When they combine and mingle, bring
A strong regard and aw: but speech alone
    Doth vanish like a flaring thing,
    And in the eare, not conscience ring.   15

Vertue

Sweet day, so cool, so calm, so bright,
The bridall of the earth and skie:
The dew shall weep thy fall to night;
        For thou must die.

Sweet rose, whose hue angrie and brave   5
Bids the rash gazer wipe his eye:
Thy root is ever in its grave,
        And thou must die.

Sweet spring, full of sweet dayes and roses,
A box where sweets compacted lie;   10
My musick shows ye have your closes,
        And all must die.

Onely a sweet and vertuous soul,
Like season'd timber, never gives;
But though the whole world turn to coal,   15
        Then chiefly lives.

Life

I made a posie, while the day ran by:
Here will I smell my remnant out, and tie
        My life within this band.
But time did beckon to the flowers, and they
By noon most cunningly did steal away,   5
        And wither'd in my hand.

My hand was next to them, and then my heart:
I took, without more thinking, in good part
      Times gentle admonition:
Who did so sweetly deaths sad taste convey,   10
Making my minde to smell my fatall day;
      Yet sugring the suspicion.

Farewell deare flowers, sweetly your time ye spent,
Fit, while ye liv'd, for smell or ornament,
      And after death for cures.   15
I follow straight without complaints or grief,
Since if my scent be good, I care not, if
      It be as short as yours.

Employment

He that is weary, let him sit.
      My soul would stirre
And trade in courtesies and wit,
      Quitting the furre
To cold complexions needing it.   5

Man is no starre, but a quick coal
      Of mortall fire:
Who blows it not, nor doth controll
      A faint desire,
Lets his own ashes choke his soul.   10

When th' elements did for place contest
      With him, whose will
Ordain'd the highest to be best,
      The earth sat still,
And by the others is opprest.   15

Life is a businesse, not good cheer;
      Ever in warres.
The sunne still shineth there or here,
      Whereas the starres
Watch an advantage to appeare.   20

Oh that I were an Orange-tree,
      That busie plant!
Then should I ever laden be,
      And never want
Some fruit for him that dressed me.   25

But we are still too young or old;
      The man is gone,
Before we do our wares unfold:
      So we freeze on,
Untill the grave increase our cold.   30

The Collar

I struck the board, and cry'd, No more.
      I will abroad.
What? shall I ever sigh and pine?
My lines and life are free; free as the road,
    Loose as the winde, as large as store.   5
      Shall I be still in suit?
Have I no harvest but a thorn
To let me blood, and not restore
What I have lost with cordiall fruit?
         Sure there was wine   10
     Before my sighs did drie it: there was corn
     Before my tears did drown it.

Is the yeare onely lost to me?
Have I no bayes to crown it?
No flowers, no garlands gay? all blasted? 15
All wasted?
Not so, my heart: but there is fruit,
And thou hast hands.
Recover all thy sigh-blown age
On double pleasures: leave thy cold dispute 20
Of what is fit, and not; forsake thy cage,
Thy rope of sands,
Which pettie thoughts have made, and made to thee
Good cable, to enforce and draw,
And be thy law, 25
While thou didst wink and wouldst not see.
Away; take heed:
I will abroad.
Call in thy deaths head there: tie up thy fears.
He that forbears 30
To suit and serve his need,
Deserves his load.
But as I rav'd and grew more fierce and wilde
At every word,
Me thought I heard one calling, *Childe*: 35
And I reply'd, *My Lord.*

The Pulley

When God at first made man,
Having a glasse of blessings standing by,
Let us (said he) poure on him all we can.
Let the world's riches, which dispersed lie,
Contract into a span. 5

So strength first made a way,
Then beautie flow'd, then wisdome, honour, pleasure.
  When almost all was out, God made a stay,
Perceiving that alone of all his treasure
    Rest in the bottome lay.   10

  For if I should (said he)
Bestow this jewell also on my creature,
  He would adore my gifts instead of me,
And rest in Nature, not the God of Nature.
    So both should losers be.   15

  Yet let him keep the rest,
But keep them with repining restlessnesse.
  Let him be rich and wearie, that at least,
If goodnesse leade him not, yet wearinesse
    May tosse him to my breast.   20

The Flower

  How fresh, O Lord, how sweet and clean
Are thy returns! Ev'n as the flowers in spring,
  To which, besides their own demean,
The late-past frosts tributes of pleasure bring.
          Grief melts away   5
          Like snow in May,
  As if there were no such cold thing.

  Who would have thought my shrivel'd heart
Could have recover'd greennesse? It was gone
  Quite under ground, as flowers depart   10
To see their mother-root when they have blown;

Where they together
All the hard weather,
Dead to the world, keep house unknown.

These are thy wonders, Lord of power,   15
Killing and quickning, bringing down to hell
    And up to heaven in an houre;
Making a chiming of a passing-bell.
            We say amisse,
            This or that is;   20
    Thy word is all, if we could spell.

O that I once past changing were,
Fast in thy Paradise, where no flower can wither!
    Many a spring I shoot up fair,
Off'ring at heav'n, growing and groaning thither;   25
            Nor doth my flower
            Want a spring-showre,
    My sinnes and I joining together.

But while I grow in a straight line,
Still upwards bent, as if heav'n were mine own,   30
    Thy anger comes, and I decline.
What frost to that? What pole is not the zone
            Where all things burn,
            When thou dost turn,
    And the least frown of thine is shown?   35

And now in age I bud again,
After so many deaths I live and write;
    I once more smell the dew and rain,
And relish versing. O my onely light,
            It cannot be   40
            That I am he
    On whom thy tempests fell all night.

These are thy wonders, Lord of love,
To make us see we are but flowers that glide.
Which when we once can finde and prove, 45
Thou hast a garden for us where to bide.
Who would be more,
Swelling through store,
Forfeit their Paradise by their pride.

Aaron

Holinesse on the head,
Light and perfections on the breast,
Harmonious bells below, raising the dead
To leade them unto life and rest.
Thus are true Aarons drest. 5

Profanenesse in my head,
Defects and darknesse in my breast,
A noise of passions ringing me for dead
Unto a place where is no rest.
Poore priest thus am I drest. 10

Onely another head
I have, another heart and breast,
Another musick, making live not dead,
Without whom I could have no rest:
In him I am well drest. 15

Christ is my onely head,
My alone onely heart and breast,
My onely musick, striking me ev'n dead;
That to the old man I may rest,
And be in him new drest. 20

So holy in my head,
    Perfect and light in my deare breast,
My doctrine tun'd by Christ, (who is not dead,
    But lives in me while I do rest)
        Come people; Aaron's drest.   25

Love

Love bade me welcome: yet my soul drew back,
    Guiltie of dust and sinne.
But quick-ey'd Love, observing me grow slack
    From my first entrance in,
Drew nearer to me, sweetly questioning,   5
    If I lack'd any thing.

A guest, I answer'd, worthy to be here:
    Love said, you shall be he.
I the unkinde, ungratefull? Ah my deare,
    I cannot look on thee.   10
Love took my hand, and smiling did reply,
    Who made the eyes but I?

Truth Lord, but I have marr'd them: let my shame
    Go where it doth deserve.
And know you not, sayes Love, who bore the blame?   15
    My deare, then I will serve.
You must sit down, sayes Love, and taste my meat:
    So I did sit and eat.

THOMAS CAREW

Song: Mediocritie In Love Rejected

Give me more love, or more disdaine;
   The Torrid, or the frozen Zone,
Bring equall ease unto my paine;
   The temperate affords me none:
Either extreame, of love, or hate,   5
Is sweeter than a calme estate.

Give me a storme; if it be love,
   Like *Danaë* in that golden showre
I swimme in pleasure; if it prove
   Disdaine, that torrent will devoure   10
My Vulture-hopes; and he's possest
Of Heaven, that's but from Hell releast:
   Then crowne my joyes, or cure my paine;
   Give me more love, or more disdaine.

To my inconstant Mistris

When thou, poore excommunicate
   From all the joyes of love, shalt see
The full reward, and glorious fate,
   Which my strong faith shall purchase me,
Then curse thine owne inconstancy.   5

A fayrer hand than thine, shall cure
  That heart, which thy false oathes did wound;
And to my soul, a soul more pure
  Than thine, shall by Loves hand be bound,
And both with equall glory crown'd.   10

Then shalt thou weepe, entreat, complain
  To Love, as I did once to thee;
When all thy teares shall be as vain
  As mine were then, for thou shalt bee
Damn'd for thy false Apostasie.   15

A deposition from Love

I was foretold, your rebell sex,
  Nor love, nor pitty knew;
And with what scorn you use to vex
  Poor hearts that humbly sue;
Yet I believ'd, to crown our pain,   5
  Could we the fortress win,
The happy Lover sure should gain
  A Paradise within:
I thought Loves plagues, like Dragons sate,
Only to fright us at the gate.   10

But I did enter, and enjoy
  What happy Lovers prove;
For I could kiss, and sport, and toy,
  And taste those sweets of love;
Which had they but a lasting state,   15

Or if in *Celia's* brest
The force of love might not abate,
   Jove were too mean a guest.
But now her breach of faith, farre more
Afflicts, than did her scorn before.   20

Hard fate! to have been once possest,
   As victor, of a heart
Achiev'd with labour, and unrest,
   And then forc'd to depart.
If the stout Foe will not resigne   25
   When I besiege a Town,
I lose, but what was never mine;
   But he that is cast down
From enjoy'd beauty, feels a woe
Only deposed Kings can know.   30

Ingratefull beauty threatned

Know *Celia*, (since thou art so proud,)
   'Twas I that gave thee thy renown:
Thou hadst, in the forgotten crowd
   Of common beauties, liv'd unknown,
Had not my verse exhal'd thy name,   5
And with it impt the wings of fame.

That killing power is none of thine,
   I gave it to thy voyce, and eyes:
Thy sweets, thy graces, all are mine;
   Thou art my star, shin'st in my skies;   10
Then dart not from thy borrowed sphere
Lightning on him that fixt thee there.

Tempt me with such affrights no more,
    Lest what I made, I uncreate:
Let fools thy mystique forms adore,   15
    I'll know thee in thy mortall state;
Wise Poets that wrapp'd Truth in tales,
Knew her themselves through all her vailes.

To Saxham

Though frost, and snow, lock'd from mine eyes
That beauty which without door lyes,
Thy gardens, orchards, walks, that so
I might not all thy pleasures know;
Yet (*Saxham*) thou within thy gate,   5
Art of thy selfe so delicate,
So full of native sweets, that bless
Thy roof with inward happiness;
As neither from, nor to thy store,
Winter takes ought, or Spring adds more.   10
The cold and frozen ayr had sterv'd
Much poore, if not by thee preserv'd;
Whose prayers have made thy Table blest
With plenty, far above the rest.
The season hardly did afford   15
Coarse cates unto thy neighbours board,
Yet thou hadst dainties, as the sky
Had only been thy Volarie;
Or else the birds, fearing the snow
Might to another deluge grow,   20
The Pheasant, Partridge, and the Lark,
Flew to thy house, as to the Ark.
The willing Oxe, of himselfe came
Home to the slaughter, with the Lamb,

And every beast did thither bring   25
Himselfe, to be an offering.
The scalie herd, more pleasure took
Bath'd in thy dish, than in the brook.
Water, Earth, Ayre, did all conspire,
To pay their tributes to thy fire,   30
Whose cherishing flames themselves divide
Through every room, where they deride
The night, and cold abroad; whilst they
Like Suns within, keep endlesse day.
Those chearfull beams send forth their light,   35
To all that wander in the night,
And seem to beckon from aloof,
The weary Pilgrim to thy roof;
Where, if refresh't he will away,
He's fairly welcome, or if stay   40
Far more, which he shall hearty find,
Both from the master, and the Hind.
The stranger's welcome, each man there
Stamp'd on his chearfull brow doth wear;
Nor doth this welcome, or his cheer   45
Grow lesse, cause he stayes longer here.
There's none observes (much less repines)
How often this man sups or dines.
Thou hast no Porter at the door
T' examin, or keep back the poor;   50
Nor locks, nor bolts; thy gates have been
Made only to let strangers in;
Untaught to shut, they doe not fear
To stand wide open all the year;
Careless who enters, for they know,   55
Thou never didst deserve a foe;
And as for theeves, thy bounty's such,
They cannot steal, thou giv'st so much.

The Inscription on the Tombe of the Lady Mary Wentworth

MARIA WENTWORTH, *Thomae Comitis Cleveland, filia praemortua prima virginiam animam exhaluit. An. Dom. 1632 Æt. suae 18.*

And here the precious dust is laid;
Whose purely-tempered Clay was made
So fine, that it the guest betray'd.

Else the soul grew so fast within,
It broke the outward shell of sin,   5
And so was hatch'd a Cherubin.

In height, it soar'd to God above;
In depth, it did to knowledge move,
And spread in breadth to general love.

Before, a pious duty shin'd   10
To Parents, courtesie behind,
On either side an equall mind.

Good to the Poor, to kindred dear,
To servants kind, to friendship clear,
To nothing but her self severe.   15

So though a Virgin, yet a Bride
To every Grace, she justifi'd
A chaste Poligamie, and dy'd.

Learn from hence (Reader) what small trust
We ow this world, where vertue must   20
Frail as our flesh crumble to dust.

An Elegie upon the Death of the Deane of Pauls, Dr. John Donne

Can we not force from widdowed Poetry,
Now thou art dead (Great DONNE), one Elegie
To crowne thy Hearse? Why yet dare we not trust
Though with unkneaded dowe-bak't prose thy dust,
Such as the uncisor'd Churchman from the flower   5
Of fading Rhetorique, short liv'd as his houre,
Dry as the sand that measures it, should lay
Upon thy Ashes, on the funerall day?
Have we no voice, no tune? Did'st thou dispense
Through all our language, both the words and sense?   10
'Tis a sad truth; The Pulpit may her plaine,
And sober Christian precepts still retaine,
Doctrines it may, and wholesome Uses frame,
Grave Homilies, and Lectures, But the flame
Of thy brave Soule, that shot such heat and light,   15
As burnt our earth, and made our darknesse bright,
Committed holy Rapes upon our Will,
Did through the eye the melting heart distill;
And the deepe knowledge of darke truths so teach,
As sense might judge, what phansie could not reach,   20
Must be desir'd for ever. So the fire,
That fills with spirit and heat the Delphique quire,
Which kindled first by thy Promethean breath,
Glow'd here a while, lies quench't now in thy death;

The Muses garden with Pedantique weedes   25
O'erspread, was purg'd by thee; The lazie seeds
Of servile imitation throwne away,
And fresh invention planted, Thou didst pay
The debts of our penurious bankrupt age;
Licentious thefts, that make poëtique rage   30
A Mimique fury, when our soules must bee
Possest, or with Anacreons Extasie,
Or Pindars, not their owne; The subtle cheat
Of slie Exchanges, and the jugling feat
Of two-edg'd words, or whatsoever wrong   35
By ours was done the Greeke, or Latine tongue,
Thou hast redeem'd, and open'd Us a Mine
Of rich and pregnant phansie, drawne a line
Of masculine expression, which had good
Old Orpheus seene, or all the ancient Brood   40
Our superstitious fooles admire, and hold
Their lead more precious than thy burnish't Gold,
Thou hadst beene their Exchequer, and no more
They each in others dust had rak'd for Ore.
Thou shalt yield no precedence, but of time,   45
And the blinde fate of language, whose tun'd chime
More charmes the outward sense; Yet thou maist claime
From so great disadvantage greater fame,
Since to the awe of thy imperious wit
Our stubborne language bends, made only fit   50
With her tough-thick-rib'd hoopes to gird about
Thy Giant phansie, which had prov'd too stout
For their soft melting Phrases. As in time
They had the start, so did they cull the prime
Buds of invention many a hundred yeare,   55
And left the rifled fields, besides the feare
To touch their Harvest, yet from those bare lands
Of what is purely thine, thy only hands

(And that thy smallest worke) have gleaned more
Than all those times, and tongues could reape before; 60
But thou art gone, and thy strict lawes will be
Too hard for Libertines in Poetrie.
They will repeale the goodly exil'd traine
Of gods and goddesses, which in thy just raigne
Were banish'd nobler Poems, now, with these 65
The silenc'd tales o'th'Metamorphoses
Shall stuffe their lines, and swell the windy Page,
Till Verse refin'd by thee, in this last Age
Turne ballad rime, or those old Idolls bee
Ador'd againe, with new apostasie; 70
Oh, pardon mee, that breake with untun'd verse
The reverend silence that attends thy herse,
Whose awfull solemne murmures were to thee
More than these faint lines, a loud Elegie,
That did proclaime in a dumbe eloquence 75
The death of all the Arts, whose influence
Growne feeble, in these panting numbers lies
Gasping short winded Accents, and so dies:
So doth the swiftly turning wheele not stand
In th'instant we withdraw the moving hand, 80
But some small time maintaine a faint weake course
By vertue of the first impulsive force:
And so whil'st I cast on thy funerall pile
Thy crowne of Bayes, Oh, let it crack a while,
And spit disdaine, till the devouring flashes 85
Suck all the moysture up, then turne to ashes.
I will not draw the envy to engrosse
All thy perfections, or weepe all our losse;
Those are too numerous for an Elegie,
And this too great, to be express'd by mee, 90
Though every pen should share a distinct part.
Yet art thou Theme enough to tire all Art;

Let others carve the rest, it shall suffice
I on thy Tombe this Epitaph incise.

> Here lies a King, that rul'd as hee thought fit   95
> The universall Monarchy of wit;
> Here lie two Flamens, and both those the best,
> Apollo's first, at last, the true Gods Priest.

To a Lady that desired I would love her

Now you have freely given me leave to love,
        What will you do?
    Shall I your mirth, or passion move,
        When I begin to woo;
Will you torment, or scorn, or love me too?   5

Each petty beauty can disdain, and I
        Spight of your hate
    Without your leave can see, and die;
        Dispence a nobler Fate!
Tis easie to destroy, you may create.   10

Then give me leave to love, & love me too
        Not with designe
    To raise, as Loves curst Rebels doe,
        When puling Poets whine,
Fame to their beauty, from their blubbr'd eyn.   15

Grief is a puddle, and reflects not clear
        Your beauties rayes;
    Joyes are pure streames, your eyes appear
        Sullen in sadder layes;
In cheerfull numbers they shine bright with prayse,   20

Which shall not mention to express you fayr,
     Wounds, flames, and darts,
    Storms in your brow, nets in your hair,
     Suborning all your parts,
Or to betray, or torture captive hearts.   25

I'll make your eyes like morning Suns appear,
     As mild, and fair;
    Your brow as Crystall smooth, and clear,
     And your dishevell'd hair
Shall flow like a calm Region of the Air.   30

Rich Nature's store, (which is the Poet's Treasure)
     I'll spend, to dress
    Your beauties, if your mine of Pleasure
     In equall thankfulness
You but unlock, so we each other bless.   35

To my worthy friend Mr. George Sandys

I presse not to the Quire, nor dare I greet
The holy Place with my unhallow'd feet:
My unwasht Muse pollutes not things Divine,
Nor mingles her prophaner notes with thine;
Here, humbly at the Porch, she listning stayes,   5
And with glad eares sucks in thy Sacred Layes.
So, devout Penitents of old were wont,
Some without doore, and some beneath the Font,
To stand and heare the Churches Liturgies,
Yet not assist the solemne Exercise.   10
Sufficeth her, that she a Lay-place gaine,

To trim thy Vestments, or but beare thy traine:
Though nor in Tune, nor Wing, She reach thy Larke,
Her Lyricke feet may dance before the Arke.
Who knowes, but that Her wandring eyes, that run   15
Now hunting Glow-wormes, may adore the Sun.
A pure Flame may, shot by Almighty Power
Into my breast the earthy flame devoure:
My Eyes, in Penitentiall dew may steepe
That brine, which they for sensuall love did weepe: 20
So (though 'gainst Natures course) fire may be quencht
With fire, and water be with water drencht.
Perhaps, my restlesse Soule, tir'd with pursuit
Of mortall beautie, seeking without fruit
Contentment there; which hath not, when enjoy'd,   25
Quencht all her thirst, nor satisfi'd, though cloy'd;
Weary of her vaine search below, above
In the first Faire may find th' immortall Love.
Prompted by thy Example then, no more
In moulds of Clay will I my God adore;   30
But teare those Idols from my heart, and Write
What his blest Sp'rit, not fond Love, shall endite.
Then, I no more shall court the Verdant Bay,
But the dry leavelesse Trunk on Golgotha:
And rather strive to gaine from thence one Thorne,   35
Than all the flourishing Wreathes by Laureats worne

A Song

Ask me no more where *Jove* bestowes,
When *June* is past, the fading rose:
For in your beauties orient deep,
These Flowers as in their causes sleep.

Ask me no more whither doe stray   5
The golden Atomes of the day:
For in pure love heaven did prepare
Those powders to inrich your hair.

Ask me no more whither doth hast
The Nightingale, when *May* is past: 10
For in your sweet dividing throat
She winters, and keeps warm her note.

Ask me no more where those starres light,
That downward fall in dead of night:
For in your eyes they sit, and there,   15
Fixed, become as in their sphere.

Ask me no more if East or West,
The Phenix builds her spicy nest:
For unto you at last she flyes,
And in your fragrant bosome dies.   20

RICHARD CRASHAW

Loves Horoscope

Love, brave Vertues younger Brother,
   Erst hath made my Heart a Mother,
   Shee consults the conscious Spheares,
   To calculate her young sons yeares.
   Shee askes if sad, or saving powers,   5
   Gave Omen to his infant howers,
   Shee askes each starre that then stood by,
   If poore Love shall live or dy.

Ah my Heart, is that the way?
   Are these the Beames that rule thy Day?   10
   Thou know'st a Face in whose each looke,
   Beauty layes ope Loves Fortune-booke;
   On whose faire revolutions wait
   The obsequious motions of Loves fate;
   Ah my Heart, her eyes and shee,   15
   Have taught thee new Astrologie.
   How e'er Loves native houres were set,
   What ever starry Synod met,
   'Tis in the mercy of her eye,
   If poore Love shall live or dye.   20

If those sharpe Rayes putting on
   Points of Death bid Love be gon,
   (Though the Heavens in counsell sate,
   To crowne an uncontrouled Fate,

Though their best Aspects twin'd upon   25
The kindest Constellation,
Cast amorous glances on his Birth,
And whisper'd the confederate Earth
To pave his paths with all the good
That warms the Bed of youth and blood;)   30
Love has no plea gainst her eye,
Beauty frownes, and Love must dye.

But if her milder influence move,
And gild the hopes of humble Love:
(Though heavens inauspicious eye   35
Lay blacke on Loves Nativitie;
Though every Diamond in *Joves* crowne
Fixt his forehead to a frowne,)
Her Eye a strong appeale can give,
Beauty smiles and Love shall live.   40

O if Love shall live, O where,
But in her Eye, or in her Eare,
In her Brest, or in her Breath,
Shall I hide poore Love from Death?
For in the life ought else can give,   45
Love shall dye, although he live.

Or if Love shall dye, O where,
But in her Eye, or in her Eare,
In her Breath, or in her Breast,
Shall I Build his funerall Nest?   50
While Love shall thus entombed lye,
Love shall live, although he dye.

The Hymn of Saint Thomas in Adoration of the Blessed Sacrament

Adoro Te

With all the powres my poor Heart hath
Of humble love and loyall Faith,
Thus low (my hidden life!) I bow to thee
Whom too much love hath bow'd more low for me.
Down down, proud sense! Discourses die.   5
Keep close, my soul's inquiring eye!
Nor touch nor taste must look for more
But each sit still in his own Door.

Your ports are all superfluous here,
Save That which lets in faith, the eare.   10
Faith is my skill. Faith can believe
As fast as love new lawes can give.
Faith is my force. Faith strength affords
To keep pace with those powrfull words.
And words more sure, more sweet, than they   15
Love could not think, truth could not say.

O let thy wretch find that reliefe
Thou didst afford the faithfull thiefe.
Plead for me, love! Allege and show
That faith has farther, here, to goe   20
And lesse to lean on. Because than
Though hid as GOD, wounds writ thee man,

Thomas might touch; None but might see
At least the suffring side of thee;
And that too was thy self which thee did cover,   25
But here ev'n That 's hid too which hides the other.

   Sweet, consider then, that I
Though allow'd nor hand nor eye
To reach at thy lov'd Face; nor can
Taste thee GOD, or touch thee MAN   30
Both yet believe; and wittnesse thee
My LORD too and my GOD, as loud as He.

   Help lord, my Faith, my Hope increase;
And fill my portion in thy peace.
Give love for life; nor let my dayes   35
Grow, but in new powres to thy name and praise.

   O dear memoriall of that Death
Which lives still, and allowes us breath!
Rich, Royall food! Bountyfull BREAD!
Whose use denyes us to the dead;   40
Whose vitall gust alone can give
The same leave both to eat and live;
Live ever Bread of loves, and be
My life, my soul, my surer selfe to mee.

   O soft self-wounding Pelican!   45
Whose breast weepes Balm for wounded man.
Ah this way bend thy benign flood
To 'a bleeding Heart that gasps for blood.
That blood, whose least drops soveraign be
To wash my worlds of sins from me.   50
Come love! Come LORD! and that long day
For which I languish, come away.

When this dry soul those eyes shall see,
And drink the unseal'd source of thee.
When Glory's sun faith's shades shall chase,   55
And for thy veil give me thy FACE.

A Hymn to the Name and Honor of the Admirable Saint Teresa

Love, thou art Absolute sole lord
Of LIFE and DEATH. To prove the word,
We'll now appeal to none of all
Those thy old Souldiers, Great and tall,
Ripe Men of Martyrdom, that could reach down   5
With strong armes, their triumphant crown;
Such as could with lusty breath
Speak loud into the face of death
Their Great LORD's glorious name, to none
Of those whose spacious Bosomes spread a throne   10
For LOVE at large to fill: spare blood and sweat;
And see him take a private seat
Making his mansion in the mild
And milky soul of a soft child.

Scarce has she learn't to lisp the name   15
Of Martyr; yet she thinks it shame
Life should so long play with that breath
Which spent can buy so brave a death.
She never undertook to know
What death with love should have to doe;   20
Nor has she e'er yet understood
Why to show love, she should shed blood;
Yet though she cannot tell you why,

She can LOVE, and she can DY.
   Scarce has she Blood enough to make   25
A guilty sword blush for her sake;
Yet has she 'a HEART dares hope to prove
How much lesse strong is DEATH than LOVE.
   Be love but there; let poor six yeares
Be pos'd with the maturest Feares   30
Man trembles at, you straight shall find
LOVE knowes no nonage, nor the MIND.
'Tis LOVE, not YEARES or LIMBS that can
Make the Martyr, or the man.
   LOVE touch't her HEART, and lo it beates   35
High, and burnes with such brave heates;
Such thirsts to dy, as dares drink up,
A thousand cold deaths in one cup.
Good reason. For she breathes All fire.
Her weake breast heaves with strong desire   40
Of what she may with fruitless wishes
Seek for amongst her MOTHER's kisses.
   Since 'tis not to be had at home
She'll travel to a Martyrdom.
No home for hers confesses she   45
But where she may a Martyr be.
   She'll to the Moores; And trade with them,
For this unvalued Diadem.
She'll offer them her dearest Breath,
With CHRIST's Name in't, in change for death.   50
She'll bargain with them; and will give
Them GOD; teach them how to live
In him: or, if they this deny,
For him she'll teach them how to DY.
So shall she leave amongst them sown   55
Her LORD's Blood; or at least her own.
   FAREWELL then, all the world! Adieu.

TERESA is no more for you.
Farewell, all pleasures, sports, and joyes,
(Never till now esteemed toyes) 60
Farewell what ever deare may bee,
MOTHER's armes or FATHER's knee,
Farewell house, and farewell home!
SHE's for the MOORS, and MARTYRDOM.

SWEET, not so fast! lo thy fair Spouse 65
Whom thou seekst with so swift vowes,
Calls thee back, and bids thee come
T'embrace a milder MARTYRDOM.

Blest powres forbid, Thy tender life
Should bleed upon a barbarous knife; 70
Or some base hand have power to race
Thy Breast's chaste cabinet, and uncase
A soul kept there so sweet, O no;
Wise heavn will never have it so.
THOU art love's victime; and must dy 75
A death more mysticall and high.
Into love's armes thou shalt let fall
A still-surviving funerall.
His is the DART must make the DEATH
Whose stroke shall taste thy hallow'd breath; 80
A Dart thrice dipt in that rich flame
Which writes thy spouse's radiant Name
Upon the roof of Heav'n; where ay
It shines, and with a soveraign ray
Beats bright upon the burning faces 85
Of soules which in that name's sweet graces
Find everlasting smiles. So rare,
So spirituall, pure, and fair
Must be th' immortall instrument
Upon whose choice point shall be sent 90
A life so lov'd; And that there be

67

Fit executioners for Thee,
The fair'st and first-born sons of fire
Blest SERAPHIM, shall leave their quire
And turn love's souldiers, upon THEE   95
To exercise their archerie.
  O how oft shalt thou complain
Of a sweet and subtle PAIN.
Of intolerable JOYES;
Of a DEATH, in which who dyes   100
Loves his death, and dyes again.
And would for ever so be slain.
And lives, and dyes; and knowes not why
To live, But that he thus may never leave to DY.
  How kindly will thy gentle HEART   105
Kisse the sweetly-killing DART!
And close in his embraces keep
Those delicious Wounds, that weep
Balsom to heal themselves with. Thus
When These thy DEATHS, so numerous,   110
Shall all at last dy into one,
And melt thy Soul's sweet mansion;
Like a soft lump of incense, hasted
By too hot a fire, and wasted
Into perfuming clouds, so fast   115
Shalt thou exhale to Heavn at last
In a resolving SIGH, and then
O what? Ask not the Tongues of men.
Angels cannot tell, suffice,
Thy selfe shall feel thine own full joyes   120
And hold them fast for ever. There
So soon as thou shalt first appear,
The MOON of maiden stars, thy white
MISTRESSE, attended by such bright
Soules as thy shining self, shall come   125

And in her first rankes make thee room;
Where 'mongst her snowy family
Immortall welcomes wait for thee.
    O what delight, when reveal'd LIFE shall stand
And teach thy lips heav'n with his hand;   130
On which thou now maist to thy wishes
Heap up thy consecrated kisses.
What joyes shall seize thy soul, when shee
Bending her blessed eyes on thee
(Those second Smiles of Heav'n) shall dart   135
Her mild rayes through thy melting heart!
    Angels, thy old friends, there shall greet thee
Glad at their own home now to meet thee.
    All thy good WORKES which went before
And waited for thee, at the door,   140
Shall own thee there; and all in one
Weave a constellation
Of CROWNS, with which the KING thy spouse
Shall build up thy triumphant browes.
    All thy old woes shall now smile on thee   145
And thy paines sit bright upon thee,
All thy sorrows here shall shine,
All thy SUFFRINGS be divine.
TEARES shall take comfort, and turn gems,
And WRONGS repent to Diadems.   150
Ev'n thy DEATHS shall live; and new
Dresse the soul that erst they slew.
Thy wounds shall blush to such bright scarres
As keep account of the LAMB's warres.
    Those rare WORKES where thou shalt leave writ,   155
Love's noble history, with wit
Taught thee by none but him, while here
They feed our soules, shall cloath THINE there.
Each heavnly word by whose hid flame

Our hard Hearts shall strike fire, the same   160
Shall flourish on thy browes, and be
Both fire to us and flame to thee;
Whose light shall live bright in thy FACE
By glory, in our hearts by grace.
   Thou shalt look round about, and see   165
Thousands of crown'd Soules throng to be
Themselves thy crown, Sons of thy vowes
The virgin-births with which thy soveraign spouse
Made fruitfull thy fair soul, goe now
And with them all about thee bow   170
To Him, put on (he'll say) put on
(My rosy love) that thy rich zone
Sparkling with the sacred flames
Of thousand soules, whose happy names
Heav'n keeps upon thy score. (Thy bright   175
Life brought them first to kisse the light
That kindled them to starrs.) and so
Thou with the LAMB, thy lord, shalt goe;
And wheresoe'er he sets his white
Steps, walk with HIM those wayes of light   180
Which who in death would live to see,
Must learn in life to dy like thee.

HENRY VAUGHAN

To Amoret gone from him

Fancy, and I, last Evening walkt,
And, *Amoret*, of thee we talkt;
The West just then had stolne the Sun,
And his last blushes were begun:
We sate, and markt how every thing   5
Did mourne his absence; How the Spring
That smil'd, and curl'd about his beames,
Whilst he was here, now check'd her streames:
The wanton Eddies of her face
Were taught lesse noise, and smoother grace;   10
And in a slow, sad channell went,
Whisp'ring the banks their discontent:
The carelesse ranks of flowers that spread
Their perfum'd bosomes to his head,
And with an open, free Embrace,   15
Did entertaine his beamy face;
Like absent friends point to the West,
And on that weake reflection feast.
If Creatures then that have no sense,
But the loose tye of influence,   20
(Though fate, and time each day remove
Those things that element their love)
At such vast distance can agree,
    Why, *Amoret*, why should not wee?

Regeneration

A ward, and still in bonds, one day
     I stole abroad,
It was high-spring, and all the way
     Primros'd, and hung with shade;
      Yet, was it frost within,   5
        And surly winds
Blasted my infant buds, and sinne
     Like Clouds ecclips'd my mind.

Storm'd thus; I straight perceiv'd my spring
      Mere stage, and show,   10
My walke a monstrous, mountain'd thing
     Rough-cast with Rocks, and snow;
      And as a Pilgrims Eye
        Far from reliefe,
Measures the melancholy skye   15
     Then drops, and rains for griefe,

So sigh'd I upwards still, at last
      'Twixt steps, and falls
I reach'd the pinacle, where plac'd
      I found a paire of scales,   20
      I tooke them up and layd
        In th' one late paines,
The other smoke, and pleasures weigh'd
     But prov'd the heavier graines:

With that, some cryed, *Away*; straight I   25
    Obey'd, and led
Full East, a faire, fresh field could spy
    Some call'd it, *Jacobs Bed*;
      A Virgin-soile, which no
        Rude feet e'er trod,   30
Where (since he stept there,) only go
    Prophets, and friends of God.

Here, I repos'd; but scarse well set,
    A grove descryed
Of stately height, whose branches met   35
    And mixt on every side;
      I entred, and once in
        (Amaz'd to see 't,)
Found all was chang'd, and a new spring
    Did all my senses greet;   40

The unthrift Sunne shot vitall gold
    A thousand peeces,
And heaven its azure did unfold
    Checqur'd with snowie fleeces,
      The aire was all in spice   45
        And every bush
A garland wore; Thus fed my Eyes
    But all the Eare lay hush.

Only a little Fountain lent
    Some use for Eares,   50
And on the dumbe shades language spent
    The Musick of her teares;
      I drew her neere, and found
        The Cisterne full
Of divers stones, some bright, and round   55
    Others ill-shap'd, and dull.

The first (pray marke,) as quick as light
    Danc'd through the flood,
But, th'last more heavy than the night
    Nail'd to the Center stood;   60
    I wonder'd much, but tir'd
        At last with thought,
My restless Eye that still desir'd
    As strange an object brought;

It was a banke of flowers, where I descried   65
    (Though 'twas mid-day,)
Some fast asleepe, others broad-eyed
    And taking in the Ray,
    Here musing long, I heard
        A rushing wind   70
Which still increas'd, but whence it stirr'd
    No where I could not find;

I turn'd me round, and to each shade
    Dispatch'd an Eye,
To see, if any leafe had made   75
    Least motion, or Reply,
    But while I listning sought
        My mind to ease
By knowing, where 'twas, or where not,
    It whisper'd *Where I please.*   80

    Lord, then said I, *On me one breath,*
    And let me dye before my death!

Cant. v 17.

*Arise O North, and come thou South-wind, and blow upon my
garden, that the spices thereof may flow out.*

The Retreate

Happy those early dayes! when I
Shin'd in my Angell-infancy.
Before I understood this place
Appointed for my second race,
Or taught my soul to fancy ought   5
But a white, Celestiall thought,
When yet I had not walkt above
A mile, or two, from my first love,
And looking back (at that short space,)
Could see a glimpse of his bright-face;   10
When on some *gilded Cloud*, or *flowre*
My gazing soul would dwell an houre,
And in those weaker glories spy
Some shadows of eternity;
Before I taught my tongue to wound   15
My Conscience with a sinfull sound,
Or had the black art to dispense
A sev'rall sinne to ev'ry sense,
But felt through all this fleshly dresse
Bright *shootes* of everlastingnesse.   20
   O how I long to travell back
And tread again that ancient track!
That I might once more reach that plaine,
Where first I left my glorious traine,
From whence th' Inlightned spirit sees   25
That shady City of Palme trees;
But (ah!) my soul with too much stay
Is drunk, and staggers in the way.

75

Some men a forward motion love,
But I by backward steps would move,   30
And when this dust falls to the urn
In that state I came return.

The Morning-Watch

O joyes! Infinite sweetness! with what flowres,
And shoots of glory, my soul breakes, and buds!
       All the long houres
       Of night, and Rest
       Through the still shrouds   5
       Of sleep, and Clouds,
    This Dew fell on my Breast;
      O how it *Blouds*,
And *Spirits* all my Earth! heark! In what Rings,
And *Hymning Circulations* the quick world   10
       Awakes, and sings;
       And rising winds,
       And falling springs,
       Birds, beasts, all things
    Adore him in their kinds.   15
       Thus all is hurl'd
In sacred *Hymnes*, and *Order*, The great *Chime*
And *Symphony* of nature. Prayer is
       The world in tune,
       A spirit-voyce,   20
       And vocall joyes
    Whose *Eccho is* heav'ns blisse.
      O let me climbe
When I lye down! The Pious soul by night
Is like a clouded starre, whose beames though said   25

To shed their light
Under some Cloud
Yet are above,
And shine, and move
Beyond that mistie shroud.   30
So in my Bed
That Curtain'd grave, though sleep, like ashes, hide
My lamp, and life, both shall in thee abide.

Peace

My Soul, there is a Countrie
   Far beyond the stars,
Where stands a winged sentrie
   All skilfull in the wars,
There above noise, and danger   5
   Sweet peace sits crown'd with smiles,
And one born in a Manger
   Commands the Beauteous files,
He is thy gracious friend,
   And (O my Soul awake!)   10
Did in pure love descend
   To die here for thy sake;
If thou canst get but thither,
   There growes the flowre of peace,
The Rose that cannot wither,   15
   Thy fortresse, and thy ease;
Leave then thy foolish ranges;
   For none can thee secure,
But one, who never changes,
   Thy God, thy life, thy Cure.   20

And do they so?

Rom. viii 19.

Etenim res Creatæ exerto Capite observantes expectant
revelationem Filiorum Dei.

And do they so? have they a Sense
    Of ought but Influence?
Can they their heads lift, and expect,
    And grone too? why th'Elect
Can do no more: my volumes said   5
    They were all dull, and dead,
They judg'd them senslesse, and their state
    Wholly Inanimate.
    Go, go; Seal up thy looks,
       And burn thy books.   10

I would I were a stone, or tree,
    Or flowre by pedigree,
Or some poor high-way herb, or Spring
    To flow, or bird to sing!
Then should I (tyed to one sure state,)   15
    All day expect my date;
But I am sadly loose, and stray
    A giddy blast each way;
    O let me not thus range!
       Thou canst not change.   20

Sometimes I sit with thee, and tarry
        An hour, or so, then vary.
Thy other Creatures in this Scene
        Thee only aim, and mean;
Some rise to seek thee, and with heads   25
        Erect peep from their beds;
Others, whose birth is in the tomb,
        And cannot quit the womb,
        Sigh there, and groan for thee,
            Their liberty.   30

O let not me do lesse! shall they
        Watch, while I sleep, or play?
Shall I thy mercies still abuse
        With fancies, friends, or newes?
O brook it not! thy blood is mine,   35
        And my soul should be thine;
O brook it not! why wilt thou stop
        After whole showres one drop?
        Sure, thou wilt joy to see
            Thy sheep with thee.   40

Corruption

Sure, It was so. Man in those early days
        Was not all stone, and Earth,
He shin'd a little, and by those weak Rays
        Had some glimpse of his birth.
He saw Heaven o'er his head, and knew from whence   5
        He came (condemned,) hither,
And, as first Love draws strongest, so from hence
        His mind sure progress'd thither.

Things here were strange unto him: Sweat, and till,
    All was a thorn, or weed,   10
Nor did those last, but (like himself,) dyed still
    As soon as they did *Seed.*
They seem'd to quarrel with him; for that Act
    That fell him, foyl'd them all,
He drew the Curse upon the world, and Crackt   15
    The whole frame with his fall.
This made him long for *home*, as loath to stay
    With murmurers, and foes;
He sigh'd for *Eden*, and would often say
    Ah! what bright days were those?   20
Nor was Heav'n cold unto him; for each day
    The valley, or the Mountain
Afforded visits, and still *Paradise* lay
    In some green shade, or fountain.
Angels lay *Leiger* here; Each Bush, and Cell,   25
    Each Oke, and high-way knew them,
Walk but the fields, or sit down at some *well*,
    And he was sure to view them.
Almighty *Love*! where art thou now? mad man
    Sits down, and freezeth on,   30
He raves, and swears to stir nor fire, nor fan,
    But bids the thread be spun.
I see, thy Curtains are Close-drawn; Thy bow
    Looks dim too in the Cloud,
Sin triumphs still, and man is sunk below   35
    The Center, and his shroud;
All's in deep sleep, and night; Thick darkness lyes
    And hatcheth o'er thy people;
But hark! what trumpets that? what Angel cries
    Arise! Thrust in thy sickle.   40

The World

I saw Eternity the other night
Like a great *Ring* of pure and endless light,
    All calm, as it was bright,
And round beneath it, Time in hours, days, years
      Driv'n by the spheres   5
Like a vast shadow mov'd, In which the world
    And all her train were hurl'd;
The doting Lover in his queintest strain
      Did there Complain,
Neer him, his Lute, his fancy, and his flights,   10
      Wits sour delights,
With gloves, and knots the silly snares of pleasure;
      Yet his dear Treasure
All scatter'd lay, while he his eyes did pour
      Upon a flowr.   15

The darksome States-man, hung with weights and woe,
Like a thick midnight-fog mov'd there so slow
    He did nor stay, nor go;
Condemning thoughts (like sad Ecclipses) scowl
      Upon his soul,   20
And Clouds of crying witnesses without
    Pursued him with one shout.
Yet digg'd the Mole, and lest his ways be found
      Workt under ground,
Where he did Clutch his prey, but one did see   25
      That policie;
Churches and altars fed him, Perjuries
      Were gnats and flies,

It rain'd about him blood and tears, but he
      Drank them as free.   30

The fearfull miser on a heap of rust
Sate pining all his life there, did scarce trust
      His own hands with the dust,
Yet would not place one peece above, but lives
      In feare of theeves.   35
Thousands there were as frantick as himself
      And hugg'd each one his pelf,
The down-right Epicure plac'd heav'n in sense
      And scornd pretence
While others slipt into a wide Excesse   40
      Said little lesse;
The weaker sort slight, triviall wares inslave
      Who think them brave,
And poor, despised truth sate Counting by`
      Their victory.   45

Yet some, who all this while did weep and sing,
And sing, and weep, soar'd up into the *Ring*,
      But most would use no wing.
O fools (said I,) thus to prefer dark night
      Before true light,   5c
To live in grots, and caves, and hate the day
      Because it shews the way,
The way which from this dead and dark abode
      Leads up to God,
A way where you might tread the Sun, and be   55
      More bright than he.
But as I did their madness so discusse
      One whisper'd thus,
This Ring the Bride-groome did for none provide
      But for his bride.   60

I John ii 16, 17.

All that is in the world, the lust of the flesh, the lust of the Eyes, and the pride of life, is not of the Father, but is of the world.
And the world passeth away, and the lusts thereof, but he that doth the will of God abideth for ever.

Man

> Weighing the stedfastness and state
> Of some mean things which here below reside,
> Where birds like watchful Clocks the noiseless date
>   And Intercourse of times divide,
> Where Bees at night get home and hive, and flowrs   5
>   Early, as well as late,
> Rise with the Sun, and set in the same bowrs;

> I would (said I) my God would give
> The staidness of these things to man! for these
> To his divine appointments ever cleave,   10
>   And no new business breaks their peace;
> The birds nor sow, nor reap, yet sup and dine,
>   The flowres without clothes live,
> Yet *Solomon* was never drest so fine.

> Man hath still either toyes, or Care,   15
> He hath no root, nor to one place is ty'd,
> But ever restless and Irregular
>   About this Earth doth run and ride,
> He knows he hath a home, but scarce knows where,
>   He sayes it is so far   20
> That he hath quite forgot how to go there.

He knocks at all doors, strays and roams,
Nay hath not so much wit as some stones have
Which in the darkest nights point to their homes,
By some hid sense their Maker gave; 25
Man is the shuttle, to whose winding quest
And passage through these looms
God order'd motion, but ordain'd no rest.

They are all gone into the world of light!

They are all gone into the world of light!
And I alone sit lingring here;
Their very memory is fair and bright,
And my sad thoughts doth clear.

It glows and glitters in my cloudy brest 5
Like stars upon some gloomy grove,
Or those faint beams in which this hill is drest,
After the Sun's remove.

I see them walking in an Air of glory,
Whose light doth trample on my days: 10
My days, which are at best but dull and hoary,
Mere glimmering and decays.

O holy hope! and high humility,
High as the Heavens above!
These are your walks, and you have shew'd them me 15
To kindle my cold love,

Dear, beauteous death! the Jewel of the Just,
  Shining no where, but in the dark;
What mysteries do lie beyond thy dust;
  Could man outlook that mark!   20

He that hath found some fledg'd birds nest, may know
  At first sight, if the bird be flown;
But what fair Well, or Grove he sings in now,
  That is to him unknown.

And yet, as Angels in some brighter dreams   25
  Call to the soul, when man doth sleep:
So some strange thoughts transcend our wonted theams,
  And into glory peep.

If a star were confin'd into a Tomb
  Her captive flames must needs burn there;   30
But when the hand that lockt her up, gives room,
  She'll shine through all the sphære.

O Father of eternal life, and all
  Created glories under thee!
Resume thy spirit from this world of thrall   35
  Into true liberty.

Either disperse these mists, which blot and fill
  My perspective (still) as they pass,
Or else remove me hence unto that hill,
  Where I shall need no glass.   40

The Night

John iii 2.

Through that pure *Virgin-shrine*,
That sacred vail drawn o'er thy glorious noon
That men might look and live as Glow-worms shine,
    And face the Moon:
  Wise *Nicodemus* saw such light   5
  As made him know his God by night.

    Most blest believer he!
Who in that land of darkness and blinde eyes
Thy long expected healing wings could see,
    When thou didst rise,   10
  And what can never more be done,
  Did at mid-night speak with the Sun!

    O who will tell me, where
He found thee at that dead and silent hour!
What hallow'd solitary ground did bear   15
    So rare a flower,
  Within whose sacred leafs did lie
  The fulness of the Deity.

    No mercy-seat of gold,
No dead and dusty *Cherub*, nor carv'd stone,   20
But his own living works did my Lord hold
    And lodge alone;
  Where *trees* and *herbs* did watch and peep
  And wonder, while the *Jews* did sleep.

Dear night! this worlds defeat;   25
The stop to busie fools; cares check and curb;
The day of Spirits; my souls calm retreat
        Which none disturb!
    Christs progress, and his prayer time;
    The hours to which high Heaven doth chime.   30

    Gods silent, searching flight:
When my Lords head is fill'd with dew, and all
His locks are wet with the clear drops of night;
        His still, soft call;
    His knocking time; The souls dumb watch,   35
    When Spirits their fair kindred catch.

    Were all my loud, evil days
Calm and unhaunted as is thy dark Tent,
Whose peace but by some *Angels* wing or voice
        Is seldom rent;   40
    Then I in Heaven all the long year
    Would keep, and never wander here.

    But living where the Sun
Doth all things wake, and where all mix and tire
Themselves and others, I consent and run   45
        To ev'ry mire,
    And by this worlds ill-guiding light,
    Erre more than I can do by night.

    There is in God (some say)
A deep, but dazling darkness; As men here   50
Say it is late and dusky, because they
        See not all clear;
    O for that night! where I in him
    Might live invisible and dim.

Quickness

False life! a foil and no more, when
      Wilt thou be gone?
Thou foul deception of all men
That would not have the true come on.

Thou art a Moon-like toil; a blinde   5
      Self-posing state;
A dark contest of waves and winde;
A mere tempestuous debate.

Life is a fix'd, discerning light,
      A knowing Joy;   10
No chance, or fit: but ever bright,
And calm and full, yet doth not cloy.

'Tis such a blissful thing, that still
      Doth vivifie,
And shine and smile, and hath the skill   15
To please without Eternity.

Thou art a toilsome Mole, or less
      A moving mist,
But life is, what none can express,
A quickness, which my God hath kist.   20

HENRY KING

The Surrender

My once dear Love; hapless that I no more
Must call thee so: the rich affections store
That fed our hopes, lies now exhaust and spent,
Like summes of treasure unto Bankrupts lent.

We that did nothing study but the way   5
To love each other, with which thoughts the day
Rose with delight to us, and with them set,
Must learn the hateful Art how to forget.

We that did nothing wish that Heav'n could give
Beyond our selves, nor did desire to live   10
Beyond that wish, all these now cancell must
As if not writ in faith, but words and dust.

Yet witness those cleer vowes which Lovers make,
Witness the chast desires that never brake
Into unruly heats; witness that brest   15
Which in thy bosom anchor'd his whole rest,
Tis no default in us, I dare acquite
Thy Maiden faith, thy purpose fair and white
As thy pure self. Cross Planets did envie
Us to each other, and Heaven did untie   20
Faster then vowes could binde. O that the Starres,
When Lovers meet, should stand oppos'd in warres!

Since then some higher Destinies command,
Let us not strive, nor labour to withstand
What is past help. The longest date of grief   25
Can never yield a hope of our relief;

And though we waste our selves in moist laments,
Tears may drown us, but not our discontents.

  Fold back our arms, take home our fruitless loves,
That must new fortunes trie, like Turtle Doves   30
Dislodged from their haunts. We must in tears
Unwind a love knit up in many years.
In this last kiss I here surrender thee
Back to thy self, so thou again art free.
Thou in another, sad as that, resend   35
The truest heart that Lover ere did lend.

  Now turn from each. So fare our sever'd hearts
As the divorc't soul from her body parts.

The Exequy

  Accept thou Shrine of my dead Saint,
Instead of Dirges this complaint;
And for sweet flowres to crown thy hearse,
Receive a strew of weeping verse
From thy griev'd friend, whom thou might'st see   5
Quite melted into tears for thee.

  Dear loss! since thy untimely fate
My task hath been to meditate
On thee, on thee: thou art the book,
The library whereon I look   10
Though almost blind. For thee (lov'd clay)
I languish out, not live the day,
Using no other exercise
But what I practise with mine eyes:
By which wet glasses I find out   15

How lazily time creeps about
To one that mourns: this, onely this
My exercise and bus'ness is:
So I compute the weary houres
With sighs dissolved into showres.   20

   Nor wonder if my time go thus
Backward and most preposterous;
Thou hast benighted me, thy set
This Eve of blackness did beget,
Who wast my day, (though overcast   25
Before thou had'st thy Noon-tide past)
And I remember must in tears,
Thou scarce had'st seen so many years
As Day tells houres. By thy cleer Sun
My love and fortune first did run;   30
But thou wilt never more appear
Folded within my Hemisphear,
Since both thy light and motion
Like a fled Star is fall'n and gon,
And twixt me and my soules dear wish   35
The earth now interposed is,
Which such a strange eclipse doth make
As ne'er was read in Almanake.

   I could allow thee for a time
To darken me and my sad Clime,   40
Were it a month, a year, or ten,
I would thy exile live till then;
And all that space my mirth adjourn,
So thou wouldst promise to return;
And putting off thy ashy shrowd   45
At length disperse this sorrows cloud.

But woe is me! the longest date
Too narrow is to calculate
These empty hopes: never shall I
Be so much blest as to descry   50
A glimpse of thee, till that day come
Which shall the earth to cinders doome,
And a fierce Feaver must calcine
The body of this world like thine,
(My Little World!); that fit of fire   55
Once off, our bodies shall aspire
To our soules bliss: then we shall rise,
And view our selves with cleerer eyes
In that calm Region, where no night
Can hide us from each others sight.   60

Mean time, thou hast her, earth: much good
May my harm do thee. Since it stood
With Heavens will I might not call
Her longer mine, I give thee all
My short-liv'd right and interest   65
In her, whom living I lov'd best:
With a most free and bounteous grief,
I give thee what I could not keep.
Be kind to her, and prethee look
Thou write into thy Dooms-day book   70
Each parcell of this Rarity
Which in thy Casket shrin'd doth ly:
See that thou make thy reck'ning streight.
And yield her back again by weight;
For thou must audit on thy trust   75
Each graine and atome of this dust,
As thou wilt answer *Him* that lent,
Not gave thee, my dear Monument.

So close the ground, and 'bout her shade
Black curtains draw, my *Bride* is laid.   80

Sleep on my *Love* in thy cold bed
Never to be disquieted!
My last good night! Thou wilt not wake
Till I thy fate shall overtake:
Till age, or grief, or sickness must   85
Marry my body to that dust
It so much loves; and fill the room
My heart keeps empty in thy Tomb.
Stay for me there; I will not faile
To meet thee in that hollow Vale.   90
And think not much of my delay;
I am already on the way,
And follow thee with all the speed
Desire can make, or sorrows breed.
Each minute is a short degree,   95
And ev'ry houre a step towards thee.
At night when I betake to rest,
Next morn I rise neerer my West
Of life, almost by eight houres saile,
Than when sleep breath'd his drowsie gale.   100

Thus from the Sun my Bottom stears,
And my dayes Compass downward bears:
Nor labour I to stemme the tide
Through which to *Thee* I swiftly glide.

'Tis true, with shame and grief I yield,   105
Thou like the *Van* first took'st the field,
And gotten hast the victory
In thus adventuring to dy
Before me, whose more years might crave
A just precedence in the grave.   110

93

But heark! My Pulse like a soft Drum
Beats my approach, tells *Thee* I come;
And slow howe'er my marches be,
I shall at last sit down by *Thee*.

   The thought of this bids me go on,   115
And wait my dissolution
With hope and comfort. *Dear* (forgive
The crime) I am content to live
Divided, with but half a heart,
Till we shall meet and never part.   120

A Contemplation upon flowers

Brave flowers, that I could gallant it like you
And be as little vaine,
You come abroad, and make a harmelesse shew,
And to your beds of Earthe againe;
You are not proud, you know your birth   5
For your Embroiderd garments are from Earth:

You doe obey your months, and times, but I
Would have it ever spring,
My fate would know no winter, never die
Nor thinke of such a thing;   10
Oh that I could my bed of Earth but view
And Smile, and looke as Chearefully as you:

Oh teach me to see Death, and not to fear
But rather to take truce;
How often have I seene you at a Bier,   15
And there look fresh and spruce;
You fragrant flowers, then teach me that my breath
Like yours may sweeten, and perfume my Death.

ANDREW MARVELL

A Dialogue between the Resolved Soul, and Created Pleasure

Courage my Soul, now learn to wield
The weight of thine immortal Shield.
Close on thy Head thy Helmet bright.
Ballance thy Sword against the Fight.
See where an Army, strong as fair,   5
With silken Banners spreads the air.
Now, if thou bee'st that thing Divine,
In this day's Combat let it shine:
And shew that Nature wants an Art
To conquer one resolved Heart.   10

PLEASURE

Welcome the Creations Guest,
Lord of Earth, and Heavens Heir.
Lay aside that Warlike Crest,
And of Nature's banquet share:
Where the Souls of fruits and flow'rs   15
Stand prepar'd to heighten yours.

SOUL

I sup above, and cannot stay
To bait so long upon the way.

On these downy Pillows lye,
Whose soft Plumes will thither fly: 20
On these Roses strow'd so plain
Lest one Leaf thy Side should strain.

SOUL

My gentler Rest is on a Thought,
Conscious of doing what I ought.

PLEASURE

If thou bee'st with Perfumes pleas'd,   25
Such as oft the Gods appeas'd,
Thou in fragrant Clouds shalt show
Like another God below.

SOUL

A Soul that knowes not to presume
Is Heaven's and its own perfume.   30

PLEASURE

Every thing does seem to vie
Which should first attract thine Eye:
But since none deserves that grace,
In this Crystal view *thy* face.

SOUL

When the Creator's skill is priz'd,   35
The rest is all but Earth disguis'd.

PLEASURE

Hark how Musick then prepares
For thy Stay these charming Aires;
Which the posting Winds recall,
And suspend the Rivers Fall.   40

SOUL

Had I but any time to lose,
On this I would it all dispose.
Cease Tempter. None can chain a mind
Whom this sweet Chordage cannot bind.

CHORUS

Earth cannot shew so brave a Sight   45
As when a single Soul does fence
The Batteries of alluring Sense,
And Heaven views it with delight.
   Then persevere: for still new Charges sound:
   And if thou overcom'st thou shalt be crown'd.   50

PLEASURE

All this fair, and soft, and sweet,
   Which scatteringly doth shine,
Shall within one Beauty meet,
   And she be only thine.

SOUL

If things of Sight such Heavens be,   55
What Heavens are those we cannot see?

PLEASURE

Where so e'er thy Foot shall go
   The minted Gold shall lie;

97

Till thou purchase all below,
   And want new Worlds to buy.   60

SOUL

Wer 't not a price who'ld value Gold?
And that's worth nought that can be sold.

PLEASURE

Wilt thou all the Glory have
   That War or Peace commend?
Half the World shall be thy Slave   65
   The other half thy Friend.

SOUL

What Friends, if to my self untrue?
What Slaves, unless I captive you?

PLEASURE

Thou shalt know each hidden Cause;
   And see the future Time: 70
Try what depth the Centre draws;
   And then to Heaven climb.

SOUL

None thither mounts by the degree
Of Knowledge, but Humility.

CHORUS

Triumph, triumph, victorious Soul;   75
The World has not one Pleasure more:
The rest does lie beyond the Pole,
And is thine everlasting Store.

On a Drop of Dew

See how the Orient Dew,
Shed from the Bosom of the Morn
  Into the blowing Roses,
Yet careless of its Mansion new;
For the clear Region where 'twas born   5
  Round in its self incloses:
  And in its little Globes Extent,
Frames as it can its native Element.
  How it the purple flow'r does slight,
    Scarce touching where it lyes,   10
  But gazing back upon the Skies,
    Shines with a mournful Light;
      Like its own Tear,
Because so long divided from the Sphear.
  Restless it roules and unsecure,   15
    Trembling lest it grow impure:
  Till the warm Sun pitty its Pain,
And to the Skies exhale it back again.
    So the Soul, that Drop, that Ray
Of the clear Fountain of Eternal Day,   20
Could it within the humane flow'r be seen,
    Remembring still its former height,
    Shuns the sweet leaves and blossoms green:
    And, recollecting its own Light,
Does, in its pure and circling thoughts, express   25
The greater Heaven in an Heaven less.
    In how coy a Figure wound,
    Every way it turns away:
    So the World excluding round,

Yet receiving in the Day. 30
  Dark beneath, but bright above:
  Here disdaining, there in Love.
How loose and easie hence to go:
How girt and ready to ascend.
Moving but on a point below, 35
It all about does upwards bend.
Such did the Manna's sacred Dew destil;
White, and intire, though congeal'd and chill.
Congeal'd on Earth: but does, dissolving, run
Into the Glories of th' Almighty Sun. 40

Bermudas

Where the remote *Bermudas* ride
In th' Oceans bosome unespy'd,
From a small Boat, that row'd along,
The listning Winds receiv'd this Song.
  What should we do but sing his Praise 5
That led us through the watry Maze,
Unto an Isle so long unknown,
And yet far kinder than our own?
Where he the huge Sea-Monsters wracks,
That lift the Deep upon their Backs. 10
He lands us on a grassy Stage;
Safe from the Storms, and Prelat's rage.
He gave us this eternal Spring,
Which here enamells every thing;
And sends the Fowls to us in care, 15
On daily Visits through the Air.
He hangs in shades the Orange bright,
Like golden Lamps in a green Night.

And does in the Pomgranates close,
Jewels more rich than *Ormus* shows.   20
He makes the Figs our mouths to meet;
And throws the Melons at our feet.
But Apples plants of such a price,
No Tree could ever bear them twice.
With Cedars, chosen by his hand,   25
From *Lebanon*, he stores the Land.
And makes the hollow Seas, that roar,
Proclaime the Ambergris on shoar.
He cast (of which we rather boast)
The Gospels Pearl upon our Coast.   30
And in these Rocks for us did frame
A Temple, where to sound his Name.
Oh let our Voice his Praise exalt,
Till it arrive at Heavens Vault:
Which thence (perhaps) rebounding, may   35
Eccho beyond the *Mexique Bay*.
Thus sung they, in the *English* boat,
An holy and a chearful Note,
And all the way, to guide their Chime,
With falling Oars they kept the time.   40

The Nymph Complaining for the Death of her Faun

The wanton Troopers riding by
Have shot my Faun and it will dye.
Ungentle men! They cannot thrive
To kill thee. Thou ne'er didst alive
Them any harm: alas nor cou'd   5
Thy death yet do them any good.

I'm sure I never wisht them ill;
Nor do I for all this; nor will:
But, if my simple Pray'rs may yet
Prevail with Heaven to forget   10
Thy murder, I will Joyn my Tears
Rather than fail. But, O my fears!
It cannot dye so. Heavens King
Keeps register of everything,
And nothing may we use in vain;   15
Even Beasts must be with justice slain,
Else Men are made their Deodands.
Though they should wash their guilty hands
In this warm life-blood, which doth part
From thine, and wound me to the Heart,   20
Yet could they not be clean: their Stain
Is dyd in such a Purple Grain.
There is not such another in
The World, to offer for their Sin.
  Unconstant *Sylvio*, when yet   25
I had not found him counterfeit,
One morning (I remember well),
Ty'd in this silver Chain and Bell,
Gave it to me: nay and I know
What he said then; I'me sure I do.   30
Said He, look how your Huntsman here
Hath taught a *Faun* to hunt his *Dear*.
But Sylvio soon had me beguil'd:
This waxed tame, while he grew wild,
And quite regardless of my smart,   35
Left me his *Faun*, but took his *Heart*.
  Henceforth I set myself to play
My solitary time away
With this: and very well content,
Could so mine idle Life have spent   40

For it was full of sport; and light
Of foot and heart; and did invite
Me to its game: it seem'd to bless
Its self in me. How could I less
Than love it? O I cannot be   45
Unkind t' a Beast that loveth me.

    Had it liv'd long, I do not know
Whether it too might have done so
As *Sylvio* did: his Gifts might be
Perhaps as false or more than he.   50
But I am sure, for ought that I
Could in so short a time espie,
Thy love was far more better then
The love of false and cruel men.

    With sweetest milk, and sugar, first   55
I it at mine own fingers nurst.
And as it grew, so every day
It wax'd more white and sweet than they.
It had so sweet a Breath! And oft
I blusht to see its foot more soft,   60
And white, (shall I say than my hand?)
Nay, any Ladies of the Land.

    It is a wond'rous thing, how fleet
'Twas on those little silver feet.
With what a pretty skipping grace,   65
It oft would challenge me the Race:
And when't had left me far away,
'Twould stay, and run again, and stay.
For it was nimbler much than Hinds;
And trod, as on the four Winds.   70

    I have a Garden of my own,
But so with Roses over grown,
And Lillies, that you would it guess
To be a little Wilderness.

And all the Spring time of the year   75
It onely loved to be there.
Among the beds of Lillyes, I
Have sought it oft, where it should lye;
Yet could not, till it self would rise,
Find it, although before mine Eyes.   80
For, in the flaxen Lillies shade,
It like a bank of Lillies laid.
Upon the Roses it would feed,
Until its Lips ev'n seem'd to bleed:
And then to me 'twould boldly trip,   85
And print those Roses on my Lip.
But all its chief delight was still
On Roses thus its self to fill:
And its pure virgin Limbs to fold
In whitest sheets of Lillies cold.   90
Had it liv'd long, it would have been
Lillies without, Roses within.

  Oh help! oh help! I see it faint:
And dye as calmely as a Saint.
See how it weeps—the Tears do come   95
Sad, slowly dropping like a Gumme.
So weeps the wounded Balsome; so
The holy Frankincense doth flow;
The brotherless Heliades
Melt in such Amber Tears as these.   100

  I in a golden Vial will
Keep these two crystal Tears, and fill
It till it do o'reflow with mine,
Then place it in *Diana's* Shrine.

  Now my Sweet Faun is vanish'd to   105
Whether the Swans and Turtles go:
In fair *Elizium* to endure,
With milk-white Lambs, and Ermins pure.

O do not run too fast: for I
Will but bespeak thy Grave, and die.　　　　110
　　First my unhappy Statue shall
Be cut in Marble; and withal,
Let it be weeping too: but there
Th'Engraver sure his Art may spare;
For I so truly thee bemoane,　　　　　　115
That I shall weep though I be Stone:
Until my Tears, still dropping, wear
My breast, themselves engraving there.
There at my feet shalt thou be laid,
Of purest Alabaster made:　　　　　　120
For I would have thine Image be
White as I can, though not as Thee.

To his Coy Mistress

　　Had we but World enough, and Time,
This coyness Lady were no crime.
We would sit down, and think which way
To walk, and pass our long Loves Day.
Thou by the *Indian Ganges* side　　　　5
Should'st Rubies find: I by the Tide
Of *Humber* would complain. I would
Love you ten years before the Flood:
And you should if you please refuse
Till the Conversion of the *Jews*.　　　　10
My vegetable Love should grow
Vaster than Empires, and more slow.
An hundred years should go to praise
Thine Eyes, and on thy Forehead Gaze.

Two hundred to adore each Breast: 15
But thirty thousand to the rest.
An Age at least to every part,
And the last Age should show your Heart.
For Lady you deserve this State;
Nor would I love at lower rate.   20
   But at my back I alwaies hear
Times winged Charriot hurrying near:
And yonder all before us lye
Desarts of vast Eternity.
Thy Beauty shall no more be found;   25
Nor, in thy marble Vault, shall sound
My ecchoing Song: then Worms shall try
That long preserv'd Virginity:
And your quaint Honour turn to dust;
And into ashes all my Lust.   30
The Grave's a fine and private place,
But none I think do there embrace.
   Now therefore, while the youthful hew
Sits on thy skin like morning [dew],
And while thy willing Soul transpires   35
At every pore with instant Fires,
Now let us sport us while we may;
And now, like am'rous birds of prey,
Rather at once our Time devour,
Than languish in his slow-chapt pow'r.   40
Let us roll all our Strength, and all
Our sweetness, up into one Ball:
And tear our Pleasures with rough strife,
Thorough the Iron gates of Life.
Thus, though we cannot make our Sun   45
Stand still, yet we will make him run.

The Fair Singer

To make a final conquest of all me,
Love did compose so sweet an Enemy,
In whom both Beauties to my death agree,
Joyning themselves in fatal Harmony;
That while she with her Eyes my Heart does bind,   5
She with her Voice might captivate my Mind.

I could have fled from One but singly fair:
My dis-intangled Soul it self might save,
Breaking the curled trammels of her hair.
But how should I avoid to be her Slave,   10
Whose subtile Art invisibly can wreath
My Fetters of the very Air I breath?

It had been easie fighting in some plain,
Where Victory might hang in equal choice.
But all resistance against her is vain,   15
Who has th'advantage both of Eyes and Voice.
And all my Forces needs must be undone,
She having gained both the Wind and Sun.

The Definition of Love

My Love is of a birth as rare
As 'tis for object strange and high:
It was begotten by Despair
Upon Impossibility.

Magnanimous Despair alone   5
Could show me so divine a thing,
Where feeble Hope could ne'er have flown
But vainly flapt its Tinsel Wing.

And yet I quickly might arrive
Where my extended Soul is fixt,   10
But Fate does Iron wedges drive,
And alwaies crowds it self betwixt.

For Fate with jealous Eye does see
Two perfect Loves; nor lets them close:
Their union would her ruine be,   15
And her Tyrannick pow'r depose.

And therefore her Decrees of Steel
Us as the distant Poles have plac'd,
(Though Loves whole World on us doth wheel)
Not by themselves to be embrac'd.   20

Unless the giddy Heaven fall,
And Earth some new Convulsion tear;
And, us to joyn, the World should all
Be cramp'd into a *Planisphere*.

As Lines so Loves *oblique* may well   25
Themselves in every Angle greet:
But ours so truly *Parallel*,
Though infinite can never meet.

Therefore the Love which us doth bind,
But Fate so enviously debars,   30
Is the Conjunction of the Mind,
And Opposition of the Stars.

Lines from

Upon Appleton House—The Garden

See how the Flowers, as at *Parade*,
Under their *Colours* stand displaid:
Each *Regiment* in order grows,
That of the Tulip, Pinke and Rose.
  But when the vigilant *Patroul*   5
Of Stars walks round about the *Pole*,
Their Leaves, that to the stalks are curl'd,
Seem to their Staves the *Ensigns* furl'd.
Then in some Flow'rs beloved Hut,
Each Bee, as Sentinel, is shut,   10
And sleeps so too: but, if once stirred,
She runs you through, or asks *the Word*.
  Oh, thou, that dear and happy Isle,
The Garden of the World erewhile,
Thou *Paradise* of four seas,   15
Which *Heaven* planted us to please,
But, to exclude the World, did guard
With watery, if not flaming Sword;
What luckless Apple did we taste,
To make us Mortal, and Thee Waste!   20
  Unhappy! shall we never more
That sweet *Militia* restore,
When gardens only had their Towrs
And all the Garrisons were Flowers:
When Roses only Arms might bear,   25
And Men did rosy garlands wear?

The Picture of little T. C. in a Prospect of Flowers

See with what simplicity
This Nimph begins her golden daies!
In the green Grass she loves to lie,
And there with her fair Aspect tames
The Wilder flow'rs, and gives them names: 5
But only with the Roses playes;
       And them does tell
What Colour best becomes them, and what Smell.

Who can foretell for what high cause
This Darling of the Gods was born!   10
Yet this is She whose chaster Laws
The wanton Love shall one day fear,
And, under her command severe,
See his Bow broke and Ensigns torn.
       Happy, who can   15
Appease this virtuous Enemy of Man!

O then let me in time compound,
And parly with those conquering Eyes;
Ere they have try'd their force to wound,
Ere, with their glancing wheels, they drive   20
In Triumph over Hearts that strive,
And them that yield but more despise.
       Let me be laid,
Where I may see thy Glories from some shade.

Mean time, whilst every verdant thing   25
It self does at thy Beauty charm,
Reform the errours of the Spring;
Make that the Tulips may have share
Of sweetness, seeing they are fair;
And Roses of their thorns disarm: 30
          But most procure
That Violets may a longer Age endure.

But O young beauty of the Woods,
Whom Nature courts with fruits and flow'rs,
Gather the Flow'rs, but spare the Buds;   35
Lest *Flora* angry at thy crime,
To kill her Infants in their prime,
Do quickly make th' Example Yours;
          And, ere we see,
Nip in the blossome all our hopes and Thee.   40

The Garden

How vainly men themselves amaze
To win the Palm, the Oke, or Bayes;
And their uncessant Labours see
Crown'd from some single Herb or Tree.
Whose short and narrow verged Shade   5
Does prudently their Toyles upbraid;
While all Flow'rs and all Trees do close
To weave the Garlands of repose.

Fair Quiet, have I found thee here,
And Innocence thy Sister dear!   10
Mistaken long, I sought you then
In busie Companies of Men.

Your sacred Plants, if here below,
Only among the Plants will grow.
Society is all but rude,   15
To this delicious Solitude.

No white nor red was ever seen
So am'rous as this lovely green.
Fond Lovers, cruel as their Flame,
Cut in these Trees their Mistress name.   20
Little, Alas, they know, or heed,
How far these Beauties Hers exceed!
Fair Trees! wheresoe'er your barkes I wound,
No Name shall but your own be found.

When we have run our Passions heat,   25
Love hither makes his best retreat.
The *Gods*, that mortal Beauty chase,
Still in a Tree did end their race.
Apollo hunted *Daphne* so,
Only that She might Laurel grow.   30
And *Pan* did after *Syrinx* speed,
Not as a Nymph, but for a Reed.

What wond'rous Life in this I lead!
Ripe Apples drop about my head;
The Luscious Clusters of the Vine   35
Upon my Mouth do crush their Wine;
The Nectaren, and curious Peach,
Into my hands themselves do reach;
Stumbling on Melons, as I pass,
Insnar'd with Flow'rs, I fall on Grass.   40

Mean while the Mind, from pleasure less,
Withdraws into its happiness:

The Mind, that Ocean where each kind
Does streight it own resemblance find;
Yet it creates, transcending these,   45
Far other Worlds, and other Seas;
Annihilating all that's made
To a green Thought in a green Shade.

Here at the Fountains sliding foot,
Or at some Fruit-trees mossy root,   50
Casting the Bodies Vest aside,
My Soul into the boughs does glide:
There like a Bird it sits, and sings,
Then whets, and combs its silver Wings;
And, till prepar'd for longer flight,   55
Waves in its Plumes the various Light.

Such was that happy Garden-state,
While Man there walk'd without a Mate:
After a Place so pure, and sweet,
What other Help could yet be meet!   60
But 'twas beyond a Mortal's share
To wander solitary there:
Two Paradises 'twere in one
To live in Paradise alone.

How well the skilful Gardner drew   65
Of flow'rs and herbes this Dial new;
Where from above the milder Sun
Does through a fragrant Zodiack run;
And, as it works, th' industrious Bee
Computes its time as well as we.   70
How could such sweet and wholsome Hours
Be reckon'd but with herbs and flow'rs!

An Horatian Ode upon Cromwel's Return from Ireland

The forward Youth that would appear
Must now forsake his *Muses* dear,
   Nor in the Shadows sing
   His Numbers languishing.
'Tis time to leave the Books in dust,   5
And oyl th' unused Armours rust:
   Removing from the Wall
   The Corslet of the Hall.
So restless *Cromwel* could not cease
In the inglorious Arts of Peace,   10
   But through adventrous War
   Urged his active Star.
And, like the three-fork'd Lightning, first
Breaking the Clouds where it was nurst,
   Did thorough his own Side   15
   His fiery way divide.
For 'tis all one to Courage high
The Emulous or Enemy;
   And with such to inclose
   Is more than to oppose.   20
Then burning through the Air he went,
And Pallaces and Temples rent:
   And *Cæsars* head at last
   Did through his Laurels blast.
'Tis Madness to resist or blame   25
The force of angry Heavens flame:
   And, if we would speak true,
   Much to the Man is due.

Who, from his private Gardens, where
He liv'd reserved and austere,   30
   As if his highest plot
   To plant the Bergamot,
Could by industrious Valour climbe
To ruine the great Work of Time,
   And cast the Kingdome old   35
   Into another Mold.
Though Justice against Fate complain,
And plead the antient Rights in vain:
   But those do hold or break
   As Men are strong or weak.   40
Nature that hateth emptiness,
Allows of penetration less:
   And therefore must make room
   Where greater Spirits come.
What Field of all the Civil Wars,   45
Where his were not the deepest Scars?
   And *Hampton* shows what part
   He had of wiser Art.
Where, twining subtile fears with hope,
He wove a Net of such a scope,   50
   That *Charles* himself might chase
   To *Caresbrooks* narrow case.
That thence the *Royal Actor* born
The *Tragick Scaffold* might adorn:
   While round the armed Bands   55
   Did clap their bloody hands.
He nothing common did or mean
Upon that memorable Scene:
   But with his keener Eye
   The Axes edge did try: 60
Nor call'd the *Gods* with vulgar spight
To vindicate his helpless Right,

But bow'd his comely Head,
Down as upon a Bed.
This was that memorable Hour   65
Which first assur'd the forced Pow'r.
   So when they did design
   The *Capitols* first Line,
A bleeding Head where they begun,
Did fright the Architects to run;   70
   And yet in that the *State*
   Foresaw its happy Fate.
And now the *Irish* are asham'd
To see themselves in one Year tam'd:
   So much one Man can do,   75
   That does both act and know.
They can affirm his Praises best,
And have, though overcome, confest
   How good he is, how just,
   And fit for highest Trust: 80
Nor yet grown stiffer with Command,
But still in the *Republick's* hand:
   How fit he is to sway
   That can so well obey.
He to the *Commons Feet* presents   85
A *Kingdome*, for his first years rents:
   And, what he may, forbears
   His Fame to make it theirs:
And has his Sword and Spoyls ungirt,
To lay them at the *Publick's* skirt.   90
   So when the Falcon high
   Falls heavy from the Sky,
She, having kill'd, no more does search,
But on the next green Bow to perch;
   Where, when he first does lure,   95
   The Falkner has her sure.

What may not then our *Isle* presume
While Victory his Crest does plume!
   What may not others fear
   If thus he crown each Year! 100
A *Cæsar* he ere long to *Gaul*,
To *Italy* an *Hannibal*,
   And to all States not free
   Shall *Clymacterick* be.
The *Pict* no shelter now shall find 105
Within his party-colour'd Mind;
   But from this Valour sad
   Shrink underneath the Plad:
Happy if in the tufted brake
The *English Hunter* him mistake; 110
   Nor lay his Hounds in near
   The *Caledonian* Deer.
But thou the Wars and Fortunes Son
March indefatigably on;
   And for the last effect 115
   Still keep thy Sword erect:
Besides the force it has to fright
The Spirits of the shady Night,
   The same *Arts* that did *gain*
   A *Pow'r* must it *maintain*. 120

ABRAHAM COWLEY

Of Wit

Tell me, O tell, what kind of thing is *Wit*,
    Thou who *Master* art of it.
For the *First matter* loves *Variety* less;
Less *Women* love 't, either in *Love* or *Dress*.
    A thousand different shapes it bears,   5
      Comely in thousand shapes appears.
Yonder we saw it plain; and here 'tis now,
Like *Spirits* in *a Place*, we know not *How*.

London that vents of *false Ware* so much store,
    In no *Ware* deceives us more.   10
For men led by the *Colour*, and the *Shape*,
Like *Zeuxes Birds* fly to the painted *Grape*;
    Some things do through our Judgment pass
      As through a *Multiplying Glass*.
And sometimes, if the *Object* be too far,   15
We take a *Falling Meteor* for a *Star*.

Hence 'tis a *Wit* that greatest *word* of *Fame*
    Grows such a common Name.
And *Wits* by our *Creation* they become,
Just so, as *Tit'lar Bishops* made at *Rome*.   20
    'Tis not a *Tale*, 'tis not a *Jest*
      Admir'd with *Laughter* at a feast,
Nor florid *Talk* which can that *Title* gain;
The *Proofs* of *Wit* for ever must remain.

'Tis not to force some lifeless *Verses* meet   25
      With their five gouty feet.
All ev'ry where, like *Mans*, must be the *Soul*,
And *Reason* the *Inferior Powers* controul.
      Such were the *Numbers* which could call
      The *Stones* into the *Theban* wall.   30
Such *Miracles* are ceast; and now we see
No *Towns* or *Houses* rais'd by *Poetrie*.

Yet 'tis not to adorn, and gild each part;
      That shows more *Cost*, than *Art*.
Jewels at *Nose* and *Lips* but ill appear;   35
Rather than *all things Wit*, let *none* be there.
      Several *Lights* will not be seen,
      If there be nothing else between.
Men doubt, because they stand so thick i' th' skie,
If those be *Stars* which paint the *Galaxie*.   40

'Tis not when two like words make up one noise;
      Jests for *Dutch Men*, and *English Boys*.
In which who finds out *Wit*, the same may see
In *An'grams* and *Acrostiques Poetrie*.
      Much less can that have any place   45
      At which a *Virgin* hides her face,
Such *Dross* the *Fire* must purge away; 'tis just
The *Author Blush*, there where the *Reader* must.

'Tis not such *Lines* as almost crack the *Stage*
      When *Bajazet* begins to rage.   50
Nor a tall *Meta'phor* in the *Bombast* way,
Nor the dry chips of short lung'd *Seneca*.
      Nor upon all things to obtrude,
      And force some odd *Similitude*.
What is it then, which like the *Power Divine*   55
We only can by *Negatives* define?

In a true piece of *Wit* all things must be,
    Yet all things there *agree*.
As in the *Ark*, joyn'd without force or strife,
All *Creatures* dwelt; all *Creatures* that had *Life*.   60
    Or as the *Primitive Forms* of all
    (If we compare great things with small)
Which without *Discord* or *Confusion* lie,
In that strange *Mirror* of the *Deitie*.

But *Love* that moulds *One Man* up out of *Two*,   65
    Makes me forget and injure you.
I took *you* for *my self* sure when I thought
That you in any thing were to be *Taught*.
    Correct my error with thy Pen;
    And if any ask me then,   70
What thing right *Wit*, and height of *Genius* is,
I'll onely shew your *Lines*, and say, *'Tis This*.

On the Death of Mr. Crashaw

Poet and *Saint*! to thee alone are given
The two most sacred *Names* of *Earth* and *Heaven*.
The hard and rarest *Union* which can be
Next that of *Godhead* with *Humanitie*.
Long did the *Muses* banisht *Slaves* abide,   5
And built vain *Pyramids* to mortal pride;
Like *Moses* Thou (though Spells and Charms withstand)
Hast brought them nobly home back to their *Holy Land*.
    Ah wretched *We*, *Poets* of *Earth*! but *Thou*
Wert *Living* the same *Poet* which thou'rt *Now*,   10
Whilst *Angels* sing to thee their ayres divine,
And joy in an applause so great as *thine*.

Equal society with them to hold,
Thou need'st not make *new Songs*, but say the *Old*.
And they (kind Spirits!) shall all rejoyce to see   15
How little less than *They*, *Exalted Man* may be.
Still the old *Heathen Gods* in *Numbers* dwell,
The *Heav'nliest* thing on Earth still keeps up *Hell*.
Nor have we yet quite purg'd the *Christian Land*;
Still *Idols* here, like *Calves* at *Bethel* stand.   20
And though *Pans Death* long since all *Oracles* breaks,
Yet still in Rhyme the *Fiend Apollo* speaks:
Nay with the worst of Heathen dotage We
(Vain men!) the *Monster Woman Deifie*;
Find *Stars*, and tie our *Fates* there in a *Face*,   25
And *Paradise* in them by whom we *lost* it, place.
What different faults corrupt our *Muses* thus?
Wanton as *Girles*, as old *Wives*, *Fabulous*!

    Thy spotless *Muse*, like *Mary*, did contain
The boundless *Godhead*; she did well disdain   30
That her *eternal Verse* employ'd should be
On a less subject than *Eternitie*;
And for a sacred *Mistress* scorn'd to take,
But her whom *God* himself scorn'd not his *Spouse* to make.
It (in a kind) *her Miracle* did do;   35
A fruitful *Mother* was, and *Virgin* too.

    How well (blest Swan) did Fate contrive thy death;
And made thee render up thy tuneful breath
In thy great *Mistress* Arms? thou most divine
And richest *Off'ring* of *Loretto's Shrine*!   40
Where like some holy *Sacrifice* t' expire,
A *Fever* burns thee, and *Love* lights the *Fire*.
Angels (they say) brought the fam'd *Chappel* there,
And bore the sacred Load in Triumph through the air.
'Tis surer much they brought thee there, and *They*,   45
And *Thou*, their charge, went *singing* all the way.

Pardon, my *Mother Church*, if I consent
That *Angels* led him when from thee he went,
For even in *Error* sure no *Danger* is
When joyn'd with so much *Piety* as *His*.   50
Ah, mighty *God*, with shame I speak 't, and grief,
Ah that our greatest *Faults* were in *Belief*!
And our weak *Reason* were ev'en weaker yet,
Rather than thus our *Wills* too strong for it.
His *Faith* perhaps in some nice Tenents might   55
Be wrong; his *Life*, I'm sure, was *in the right*.
And I my self a *Catholick* will be,
So far at least, great *Saint*, to *Pray* to thee.
    Hail, *Bard Triumphant*! and some care bestow
On *us*, the *Poets Militant* Below!   60
Oppos'ed by our old En'emy, adverse *Chance*,
Attack'ed by *Envy*, and by *Ignorance*,
Enchain'd by *Beauty*, tortur'd by *Desires*,
Expos'd by *Tyrant-Love* to savage *Beasts* and *Fires*.
Thou from low earth in nobler *Flames* didst rise,   65
And like *Elijah*, mount *Alive* the skies.
Elisha-like (but with a wish much less,
More fit thy *Greatness*, and my *Littleness*)
Lo here I beg (I whom thou once didst prove
So humble to *Esteem*, so Good to *Love*)   70
Not that thy *Spirit* might on me *Doubled* be,
I ask but *Half* thy mighty *Spirit* for Me.
And when my *Muse* soars with so strong a Wing,
'Twill learn of things *Divine*, and first of *Thee* to sing.

Hymn: to light

First born of *Chaos*, who so fair didst come
    From the old *Negro's* darksome womb!
    Which when it saw the lovely Child,
The melancholly Mass put on kind looks and smil'd,

Thou Tide of Glory which no Rest dost know,   5
    But ever Ebb, and ever Flow!
    Thou Golden shower of a true Jove!
Who does in thee descend, and Heav'n to Earth make Love!

Hail active Natures watchful Life and Health!
    Her Joy, her Ornament, and Wealth!   10
    Hail to thy Husband Heat, and Thee!
Thou the worlds beauteous Bride, and lusty Bridegroom He!

Say from what Golden Quivers of the Sky,
    Do all thy winged Arrows fly?
    Swiftness and Power by Birth are thine: 15
From thy Great Sire they came, thy Sire the word Divine

'Tis, I believe, this Archery to show,
    That so much cost in Colours thou,
    And skill in Painting dost bestow,
Upon thy ancient Arms, the Gawdy Heav'nly Bow.   20

Swift as light Thoughts their empty Carriere run,
    Thy Race is finisht, when begun,
    Let a Post-Angel start with Thee,
And Thou the Goal of Earth shalt reach as soon as He:

Thou in the Moons bright Chariot proud and gay,   25
    Dost thy bright wood of Stars survay;
    And all the year dost with thee bring
Of thousand flowry Lights thine own Nocturnal Spring.

Thou *Scythian*-like dost round thy Lands above
    The Suns gilt Tent for ever move,   30
    And still as thou in pomp dost go
The shining Pageants of the World attend thy show.

Nor amidst all these Triumphs dost thou scorn
    The humble Glow-worms to adorn,
    And with those living spangles gild,   35
(O Greatness without Pride!) the Bushes of the Field.

Night, and her ugly Subjects thou dost fright,
    And sleep, the lazy Owl of Night;
    Asham'd and fearful to appear
They screen their horrid shapes with the black Hemisphere.   40

With 'em there hastes, and wildly takes the Alarm,
    Of painted Dreams, a busie swarm,
    At the first opening of thine eye,
The various Clusters break, the antick Atomes fly.

The guilty Serpents, and obscener Beasts   45
    Creep conscious to their secret rests:
    Nature to thee does reverence pay;
Ill Omens, and ill Sights removes out of thy way.

At thy appearance, Grief it self is said,
    To shake his Wings, and rowse his Head.   50
    And cloudy care has often took
A gentle beamy Smile reflected from thy Look.

At thy appearance, Fear it self grows bold;
    Thy Sun-shine melts away his Cold.
      Encourag'd at the sight of Thee,   55
To the cheek Colour comes, and firmness to the knee.

Even Lust the Master of a hardned Face,
    Blushes if thou beest in the place,
      To darkness' Curtains he retires,
In Sympathizing Night he rolls his smoaky Fires.   60

When, Goddess, thou liftst up thy wakened Head,
    Out of the Mornings purple bed,
      Thy Quire of Birds about thee play,
And all the joyful world salutes the rising day.

The Ghosts, and Monster Spirits, that did presume   65
    A Bodies Priv'lege to assume,
      Vanish again invisibly,
And Bodies gain agen their visibility.

All the Worlds bravery that delights our Eyes
    Is but thy sev'ral Liveries,   70
      Thou the Rich Dye on them bestowest,
Thy nimble Pencil Paints this Landskape as thou go'st.

A Crimson Garment in the Rose thou wear'st;
    A Crown of studded Gold thou bear'st,
      The Virgin Lillies in their White,   75
Are clad but with the Lawn of almost Naked Light.

The Violet, springs little Infant, stands,
    Girt in thy purple Swadling-bands:
      On the fair Tulip thou dost dote;
Thou cloath'st it in a gay and party-colour'd Coat.   80

With Flame condenst thou dost the Jewels fix,
    And solid Colours in it mix:
    Flora her self envyes to see
Flowers fairer than her own, and durable as she.

Ah, Goddess! would thou could'st thy hand withhold,   85
    And be less Liberall to Gold;
    Didst thou less value to it give,
Of how much care (alas) might'st thou poor Man relieve!

To me the Sun is more delightful far,
    And all fair Dayes much fairer are.   90
    But few, ah wondrous few there be,
Who do not Gold prefer, O Goddess, ev'n to Thee.

Through the soft wayes of Heaven, and Air, and Sea,
    Which open all their Pores to Thee;
    Like a cleer River thou dost glide,   95
And with thy Living Stream through the close Channels slide.

But where firm Bodies thy free course oppose,
    Gently thy source the Land o'erflowes;
    Takes there possession, and does make,
Of Colours mingled, Light, a thick and standing Lake.   100

But the vast Ocean of unbounded Day
    In th' Empyraean Heaven does stay.
    Thy Rivers, Lakes, and Springs below
From thence took first their Rise, thither at last must Flow.

COMMENTARY AND NOTES

JOHN DONNE

LIFE

John Donne was born in London in 1572. His parents were Roman Catholics, and he was brought up in that faith, fully aware of its attendant dangers and difficulties in those times. 'I had my first breeding and conversation', he wrote later, 'with men of afflicted and suppressed religion, accustomed to the despite of death and hungry of an imagin'd Martyrdome.' His father was a prosperous ironmonger; and his mother was the daughter of John Heywood the dramatist, the granddaughter of the sister of Sir Thomas More (who was executed by Henry VIII for his adherence to Papal supremacy), and the sister of Jasper Heywood, a Jesuit missionary priest.

When Donne was four his father died. At the age of twelve he went up to Oxford, where he studied until his seventeenth year; being a Catholic, however, he was unable to take a degree. Izaak Walton (who in Donne's later years was his friend and parishioner, and to whose biography of Donne we are chiefly indebted for our knowledge of his life) states that after leaving Oxford, Donne went on to Cambridge, but there is no proof of this. It seems highly probable that he spent the next few years travelling abroad, in Italy and Spain.

We next hear of him as a law student at the Inns of Court in London. He entered Thavie's Inn in 1591, and transferred to Lincoln's Inn in May 1592. In 1593 his younger brother, Henry, was imprisoned at Newgate for harbouring a priest, and died of gaol fever. During this year Donne came of age, and received his own and his brother's share of their father's estate.

From 1592 to 1596, the years of his residence at Lincoln's Inn, Donne lived the life of a brilliant young man about town. An acquaintance recalled him as 'not dissolute but very neat: a great visiter of ladies, a great frequenter of plays, a great writer of conceited verses'. During this period many of the *Songs and Sonets* must have been written, and the love affairs they deal with must have taken place. The poems were not published but circulated in manuscript, and Donne rapidly gained a reputation as a poet in the circles he frequented.

We must not think of Donne, however, as an idle debauchee. Avid of pleasure, he was also avid of learning and ideas, as his poems show. Walton says that he studied every morning from 4 a.m. till 10, though he admits that 'he took great liberty after it'. The nature of his studies is significant. According to Walton, 'he, being then unresolved what Religion to adhere to . . . did . . . presently lay aside all study of the Law . . . and begin seriously to survey, and consider the Body of Divinity, as it was then controverted betwixt the *Reformed* and the *Roman Church* . . .' and Donne confirms this in his Preface to his *Pseudo-Martyr* (1610). This study of divinity was no doubt motivated by Donne's lifelong passion for truth; but we may safely assume, I believe, that it was also prompted by the difficulties of his own position and prospects. His brother had died as a result of his faith; and Donne, a man of great ability and corresponding ambition, could hope for no public preferment in England if he remained a Catholic. He was too honest simply to abandon his faith for worldly reasons; so what more natural than that he should examine its basis critically? Eventually, after several years, he conformed to the Anglican faith; but his conversion was not sudden or spectacular, and certain doubts remained with him for a long time.

In 1596 he sailed with the Earl of Essex's expedition to Cadiz, and in 1597 with that to the Azores. Soon after his return he became private secretary to Sir Thomas Egerton, Keeper of the Great Seal and Lord High Chancellor. By this time, his final decision to embrace the Anglican faith must have been made. As Egerton's secretary, he was extremely successful —Egerton later described him as 'such a Secretary as was fitter to serve a King than a Subject'; and a distinguished career in public life seemed open to him. After five years, however, he took a step which utterly ruined his prospects of secular advancement and changed the whole course of his life. He secretly married the seventeen-year-old niece of Lady Egerton, Anne More, for whom some of his finest love poems were written.

When the news was broken to Sir George More, Anne's father, he was furiously angry. He compelled Egerton to dismiss Donne, carried Anne off to his house in Surrey, and had Donne imprisoned. After his release, Donne had to engage in an expensive lawsuit to obtain possession of his wife, using up his scanty financial resources. Thereafter, a partial reconciliation with Sir George followed; he requested Egerton to reinstate Donne, but Egerton, though he had dismissed him reluctantly, refused. For several years Donne lived a life of anxiety and comparative penury, maintaining his rapidly growing family on his wife's allowance from her father and the bounty of relatives or of eminent people whose patronage he was forced to pay for by writing adulatory verse. He cultivated influential people, hoping through their influence to obtain at last some worthy employment in the State, but without success.

Indeed, Donne seems unwittingly to have frustrated his own designs. For some years he assisted Thomas Morton (later Bishop of Durham), one of James I's favourite chaplains, in religious controversy designed to convert the English Roman Catholics, an activity for which Donne's study of religious differences equipped him admirably. Both Morton and the King were so impressed by his ability that they pressed him to enter the Church. Walton says that it was at the King's command that Donne wrote his *Pseudo-Martyr* (1610), in which he castigated the recusants as sham martyrs. Though Donne continued to press for a secular post, the King made up his mind, despite Donne's protests of unworthiness, that divinity was his destined profession, and eventually said, when the Earl of Somerset requested Donne's appointment to a Clerkship to the Council: 'I know Mr. Donne . . . has the abilities of a learned Divine; and will prove a powerful Preacher, and my desire is to prefer him that way, and in that way, I will deny you nothing for him.' Soon afterwards, Donne bowed to the inevitable. He was ordained in January 1615, gained rapid preferment, and became Dean of St. Paul's in 1621.

A great deal of Donne's behaviour between his marriage and his entry into holy orders seems extremely worldly, and one is tempted to conclude that the way in which he used his learning and skill in controversy to impress James was a hypocritical device to gain secular employment— that he cared little for theology save as a means to an end. But such a conclusion is far from the truth. Donne was always a paradoxical character, and his motives may have been mixed; but from about 1606 onwards he began to write religious poems of deep sincerity, though at the same time he was writing adulatory verse-epistles to various noble ladies. Moreover, both his temperament and his difficulties subjected him to fits of depression and melancholy; and he thought and wrote profoundly of the vanity of the worldly and temporal in contrast to the eternal and divine.

Devious though the paths were that led Donne to the church, there is no doubt of his devotion to it from the time he took holy orders. His wife's death in childbirth in 1617 almost overwhelmed him with grief, and thereafter his ministry was his sole remaining passion. During the remaining ten years of his life after his appointment as Dean of St. Paul's he became the most famous preacher of his day. Not only his religious poems but also his sermons are among the glories of English literature; and he brought to both all the intelligence and passion, all the magnificent intensity and subtlety of expression, that had earlier characterized his *Songs and Sonets*. Nearly everything he wrote and said during these years was sombre and austere. He deeply repented the excesses of his youth, and was much preoccupied by death.

He died on 31st March 1631. Knowing he was dying, he had a statue made of himself dressed in his shroud, which he kept by his bedside so that he might meditate on it. Having put all his affairs in order, Walton says, '. . . as his soul ascended, and his last breath departed from him, he closed his own eyes, and then disposed of his hands and body into such a posture as required not the least alteration by those that came to shroud him.'

POETRY

The characteristics of Donne's poetry are largely dealt with in the general Introduction to this volume, for he is the archetypal Metaphysical poet. As for his greatness, that derives from the power of his mind and imagination, the force and depth of his emotions, his power to express himself in words of a vividness and an immediacy that sometimes recall Shakespeare (Shakespearean, too, is his tendency to cram meaning into his lines until it is almost more than they can carry), and his extraordinary skill in versification. These qualities the reader will see for himself. There are, however, two points to be stressed here.

The first concerns his originality. We must not forget that Donne was an Elizabethan; and typical Elizabethan poetry, largely modelled on Petrarch and Spenser, was characterized by smooth regularity of verse, conventional ornament and imagery, and conventional themes. It was consciously artificial and rhetorical, and often written to be sung, which limited its range of mood and precluded the flexibility of movement that suggests the speaking voice. Such poetry continued to be written and published long after Donne had begun to write—his influence was at first greatly limited because his poems, most of which were not published until after his death, were known only to the comparatively small circle of acquaintances who saw them in manuscript. Dramatic blank verse, notably Shakespeare's, moved towards greater realism; but in non-dramatic poetry it was Donne who established a new mode. His verse is colloquial in diction, suggestive of speech in movement, and free from decorative elaboration, drawing its imagery not from conventional sources, but from any material that suggested itself, and sometimes dispensing with imagery altogether. Moreover, the feelings and ideas expressed by Donne's verse are quite different from the conventional themes of the Petrarchan sonneteers. His psychology is realistic and subtle. His love poems passionately analyse the relationship of love in all its aspects, pleasant and otherwise; and later, in his divine poems, the same passionate analysis is applied to religious themes, notably the relationship between God and man.

The second point to be stressed is the *range* of Donne's work. All the poems printed here are famous, but they are no more than a token representation of his work, and nearly all of them are short. The interested reader (and I cannot imagine any intelligent and sensitive reader failing to find Donne interesting) is recommended to extend his experience by turning to James Reeves's excellent *Selected Poems of John Donne* in this series, and thereafter to read the longer poems, the *Satyres* and the two *Anniversaries: An Anatomie of the World* and *Of the Progresse of the Soul*.

Notes on the Poems of John Donne

11. THE GOOD-MORROW

This fine poem illustrates most of Donne's characteristics. The movement, involving a complicated stanza form, achieves the effect of speech (notice how naturally such words as *did* and *wean'd* in *l*.2 are stressed); the language is vigorous, colloquial and concrete (*suck'd*, *snorted*); the imagery is drawn from many sources; and the whole poem expresses both passion and subtle intellectual activity.

l.4 Seven young Christians of Ephesus, fleeing from the persecution of Decius in A.D. 250, were said to have hidden in a cavern and slept there for 187 years.

l.19. It was thought that compounds of which the ingredients were equal to each other could not be dissolved.

12. THE SUNNE RISING

The vigorous opening typifies the dramatic element in Donne's verse and his tendency deliberately to surprise the reader by an unexpected mode of expression.

l.9. *Love, all alike:* love, which never changes.

ll.11–12. What makes you think your beams are all-powerful?

l.17.   *both the'India's of spice and Myne:* the East Indies (famous for spices
and the West Indies (famous for gold).

l.30.   *spheare:* the sun was thought to be carried on one of a system of con-
centric spheres, of which the earth was the centre, in Ptolemaic astronomy.
The moon and the other heavenly bodies also had their spheres.

13.   SONG: SWEETEST LOVE, I DO NOT GOE

This lovely poem was probably, like *A Valediction: forbidding mourning*,
written for his wife, when Donne went to the Continent in 1611. According
to Walton, she said that 'Her divining soul boded her some ill in his absence',
and begged him not to leave her.

The poem's movement shows that when Donne wrote 'harshly', it was
not because he could not help it but because he wished to. Here his verse is as
mellifluous as any Elizabethan lyric; nevertheless it is not divorced from
speech.

ll.33–36.   Do not let your prophetic heart forecast any misfortune for me,
for if you do, Fate may make your fears come true.

14.   THE ANNIVERSARIE

Stanza 2: When we die, our bodies will be separated, but our souls,
which contain only love, will unite and prove our love, which will perhaps
become even greater than it is now.

l.18.   *inmates:* lodgers, visitors.

15.   TWICKNAM GARDEN

Donne does not tell us what the *disgrace* (*l*.14) is, but I surmise, from the
last line of the poem, that he is bitter because some married woman whom
he expected to return his love for her has decided to be 'true' to her husband.

ll.3–4.   The sights and sounds of this garden would comfort any woe, if it
were not for the fact that . . .

l.17.   *mandrake:* mandragora, of which the root was supposed to be shaped
like a man and to scream when pulled up.

l.21.   *try your mistresse Teares:* test your mistress's tears.

16.   A VALEDICTION: OF WEEPING

Donne is about to go overseas, and this poem expresses the grief of parting.
The poem is a series of Metaphysical conceits.

l.3.   *thy stampe they beare:* they reflect your face.

l.8.   *that thou:* that image of you.

l.9.   You and I, when in different countries, are nothing, since our tears
can no longer reflect each other's faces.

l.20.   *spheare:* see note to *The Sunne Rising*, *l*.30.

17. A NOCTURNALL UPON S. LUCIES DAY

This poem expresses the death of the soul occasioned by the loss of some woman he loved. Grierson observes of it that it illustrates Donne's power 'to produce an intense impression by the most abstract means'. Observe the deliberately nerveless quality of the movement, which enacts the feeling of hopelessness.

*l.*15.　*quintessence:* the pure and concentrated essence, obtained by distillation.

*l.*18.　*things which are not:* negations.

*l.*21.　*limbecke:* a vessel used for distilling.

*l.*29.　*Elixer:* another word for *quintessence.*

*ll.*30–31.　If I were a man, I should certainly know that I were.

*l.*34.　*invest:* possess, enclose within themselves.

*l.*38.　*the lesser Sunne:* Donne's *Sunne* was his beloved, who is dead. The real sun is less than she.

*l.*39.　*the Goat:* one of the signs of the zodiac, and a symbol of lust.

19. A VALEDICTION: FORBIDDING MOURNING (See note on SONG)

*l.*11.　*trepidation of the spheares:* an astronomical expression relating to the movement of the axis of the earth in relation to the sun which was formerly thought to cause the precession of the equinoxes (the slow but continual shifting of the equinoctial points from east to west). The general sense is that earthquakes cause alarm, but the movement of the universe, though greater, does not. By analogy, 'ordinary' lovers may fear and lament their separation, but we, who are superior to them, can take ours calmly, for we are never really parted.

*l.*35.　*just:* exact.

20. THE EXTASIE

This remarkably subtle work is perhaps the most famous of Donne's love poems; certainly no one else could have written it. With his characteristic blend of passion and ratiocination, he here seeks to convey his sense of the interdependence of the spiritual and the physical in love. Notice the extraordinary range of the imagery—from theories on the nature of souls to the threading of beads on a string and the transplanting of a violet.

Extasie: a temporary departure of the soul from the body.

*ll.*9–10.　Holding hands was as yet our only physical union.

*ll.*11–12.　All we begot, or propagated, was the image of each in the other's eyes.

*l.*17.　*negotiate:* negotiated, parleyed.

*l.*27.　might take on a purer essence, a further refinement (v. *l.*21) from listening to the speech of our souls.

ll.31–32. By this ecstasy we see that it was not sex that caused us to love each other: we see that we were previously unaware of the true source of our love.

ll.41–44. The union of two souls produces a single soul which is superior to the originals and without their faults.

ll.51–52. *Wee are . . . spheare:* our united bodies are the sphere in which our two souls meet and command.

l.55. Whereas the *force* (faculty or function) of the soul is perception, the *forces* of the body are the senses. Without the senses (which the body yields to, or puts at the disposal of, the soul) the soul could not perceive.

l.56. *allay:* alloy—an inferior metal, mixed with one of greater value. The body is inferior to the soul, but a necessary adjunct: it is not worthless dross.

ll.57–60. Just as heavenly bodies influence men through the medium of air (as was believed), so our souls are united through the medium of our bodies.

ll.61–68. The blood was thought to produce three kinds of *spirits*—natural, vital and animal—and these were a sort of medium between soul and body. 'The spirits in a man which are the thin and active part of the blood, and so are of a kind of middle nature, between soul and body, those spirits are able to doe, and they doe the office, to unite and apply the faculties of the soul to the organs of the body, and so there is a man.' (Donne Sermon XXVI.) The analogy is that the souls of lovers cannot communicate and express their love without the medium of the body.

23. THE FUNERALL

Typical of Donne's preoccupation with physical death (a preoccupation common in Jacobean literature). He imagines himself being buried with a bracelet of his mistress's hair on his arm. Note the bitter joke in the last line.

l.3. *subtile:* fine, thin.

l.22. to allow it the properties of his soul; take it as a symbol of his soul.

l.23. *bravery:* pride, the opposite of *humility* (*l*.21).

24. ELEGIE V. HIS PICTURE

Probably written for his mistress when he set off on the expedition to Cadiz in 1596. An example of graphic description, and of Donne's 'rugged' handling of the heroic couplet. Observe how the irregularity of such a line as *l*.9 helps to convey its sense.

ll.3–4. My picture is a shadow. If I die, and thus become a shadow, it will resemble me even more than it does now.

l.19. *who:* love (*l*.18).

l.20. *to disused tastes:* to the taste of those who are not used to it.

This was probably written while Donne was studying the rival claims of the Roman and Anglican churches, about 1593 to 1594. It is probably modelled on the style of the Latin satirist *Persius*, noted for harshness of style. The harshness of Donne's lines is therefore deliberate, and produces a sinewy force and what Dr. F. R. Leavis calls 'a mimetic flexibility' that has affinities with Shakespeare's dramatic blank verse. Yet Donne is using the heroic couplet.

The conclusion that Donne reaches in this poem is that the true religion is that which is nearest to the Primitive Church. Donne was still far from being a convinced Anglican at this time.

l.1. *spleene:* anger.

brave: proud.

l.9. *them:* people of 'the first blinded age'.

l.11. *blinde Philosophers:* the philosophers of pagan times who, while 'blind' in the sense that they did not know Christianity, had nevertheless a strict code of morality.

l.17. *mutinous Dutch:* the Dutch were rebelling against their Spanish overlords.

l.23. *Salamanders:* lizard-like animals which were supposed to be able to live in fire.

l.24. *the line:* the equator.

l.25. the countries near the equator distil our bodies into sweat (*limbecks:* see note on *A Nocturnall upon S. Lucies day, l.21*).

ll.34–35. *would allow thee faine, his whole Realme to be quit:* would gladly allow thee the freedom of his whole realm.

l.66. *divers:* diverse.

l.70. *of force:* perforce, of necessity.

and forc'd but one: and of necessity only one.

l.77. *in strange way:* on a strange road.

l.85. *to will:* to intend.

ll.86–87. 'Hard deeds are achieved by the body's pains or efforts and hard knowledge attained to by the mind's' (Grierson).

l.92. The kings who, under pretence of religion, kill those they hate are not vicars (deputies) of God, as they claim, but hangmen in the service of Fate.

ll.96–97. Philip of Spain, Pope Gregory, Henry VIII, or Martin Luther.

28. HOLY SONNETS

I

This and the next three poems are among the finest of Donne's *Holy*

Sonnets, and among the finest sonnets in the language. Together with the two final poems, they were written after the death of his wife in 1617.
l.8. by sinne in it: by reason of the sin it contains. See Psalm xxxviii, 3.
l.14. Adamant: the loadstone.

VII
Donne imagines first the Day of Judgment.
l.5. All who were drowned in the Flood (Noah's) and who shall die by the fire that will consume the world on the last day.

X
ll.5–6. Since we get much pleasure from rest and sleep, which are only imitations of death, we shall get even more from death itself.

XIV
This sonnet is notable for the flexibility with which Donne handles his metre, the use he makes of the sounds of words, and the range of the imagery.

30. HYMNE TO GOD MY GOD, IN MY SICKNESSE
No poem that Donne ever wrote is more typical, than this, which was written during his sickness in 1623.
l.10. per fretum febris: by the straits of fever. The derivation of *fretum* also suggests 'seething' or 'boiling', an association with heat appropriate to fever.
streights: a pun, meaning (i) 'channel', (ii) 'distress' or 'circumstances of hardship'.
l.11. my West: i.e. where my sun (my life) shall set.
ll.16–19. 'Be my home in the Pacific, or in the East Indies, or in Jerusalem, —to each I must sail through a strait, viz. Anyan (i.e. Behring) Strait if I go west by the North-West passage, or Magellan (for the route round Cape Horn was unknown), or Gibraltar.' (Grierson.)
ll.21–22. An old belief.
l.26. purple: the colour of kingly robes (he is thinking of Christ as king), and (often, in poetry) of blood. When the Roman soldiers mocked Christ, 'they stripped him, and put on him a scarlet robe. And when they had platted a crown of thorns, they put it upon his head . . . and mocked him, saying, Hail, King of the Jews!' (Matth. xxvii, 28–29).

31. A HYMNE TO GOD THE FATHER
In this poem, Donne puns on his own name. As with the puns in the previous poem he finds no inconsistency between punning and the most solemn thoughts. Izaak Walton says that Donne caused this hymn 'to be set

to a most grave and solemn Tune, and to be often sung to the *Organ* by the *Choristers* of St. *Paul's* Church, in his own hearing . . . and . . . did occasionally say to a friend, *The words of this* Hymn *have restored to me the same thoughts of joy that possest my Soul in my sickness when I composed it. And, O the power of Church-musick! that Harmony added to this Hymn has raised the Affections of my heart, and quickened my graces of zeal and gratitude . . .'*

GEORGE HERBERT

LIFE

George Herbert was born on 3rd April 1593, the fifth son of Richard and Magdalen Herbert. His family, the elder branch of which held the Earldom of Pembroke, was the most distinguished and powerful of the Welsh Marches. He was born at or near Montgomery Castle (of which the Herberts were hereditary governors). Richard Herbert died when George was three and a half, leaving seven sons and three daughters, whose upbringing now became their mother's chief care. Magdalen Herbert was a woman of great character, intelligence, piety and beauty; and her influence on George Herbert's life was very strong.

In 1604 the family moved to London. It was probably about this time that John Donne became acquainted with Mrs. Herbert. She helped and encouraged him during his difficulties after his imprudent marriage, and their friendship lasted until her death in 1627. In his sermon at her funeral, Donne paid glowing tribute to her excellent qualities and described her house as 'a court in conversation of the best'. Donne undoubtedly encouraged Herbert both in his poetry and in his ultimate decision to take holy orders.

When he was twelve Herbert entered Westminster School, and after a year there was nominated a King's Scholar. His school career was extremely successful: his headmaster's parting exhortation to him forecast that he 'would not fail to arrive at the top of learning in any *Art* or *Science*', and also warned him against impairing his health by too much study—for despite all his other advantages Herbert suffered ill-health throughout his life, and frequently mentions it in his letters and poems. While Herbert was at Westminster, his mother married Sir John Danvers, a rich, handsome and cultured man much younger than herself. Danvers, brother of the Earl of Danby, was a friend and favourite of the Lord Chancellor, Francis Bacon, whose friend Herbert himself became. George's relations with his stepfather were always very good.

In 1609 Herbert entered Trinity College, Cambridge. Shortly afterwards he sent his mother two sonnets, declaring 'that my poor Abilities in *Poetry* shall be all, and ever consecrated to God's glory'—a resolution to which he adhered throughout his life.

His mother wished Herbert to enter the Church, and he appears to have intended this himself when he went up to Cambridge. He quickly made a success of academic life, however, and became attracted by the prospects of distinction that university office held. He was elected a minor Fellow of his college in 1614, and a major Fellow in March 1615/16, and proceeded to the master's degree in 1616. Thereafter, he pursued his studies in classics and divinity, and was given a minor college office which involved a little teaching. Izaak Walton says of him (in his *Life of George Herbert*) at about this period that 'if during this time he exprest any Error, it was that he kept himself too much retir'd, and at too great a distance with all his inferiours: and his cloaths seem'd to prove, that he put too great a value on his parts and Parentage.'

In 1618 he was appointed to his first university office as Praelector, or Reader in Rhetoric. He was required to lecture four or five mornings a week, expounding in English such classical orators as Cicero or Quintilian. However, he chose to lecture in fulsomely flattering terms on a Latin oration of King James's, which suggests what shape his ambitions were taking. Before the end of his year's duty as Praelector he was aspiring to succeed the retiring Public Orator, for whom he had already deputised at least once. This post offered opportunities for contact with the King and other people of the highest importance, and could lead to appointment to high office in the State. Herbert made use of all the influence available to him to obtain it, and in January 1619/20 he was elected to the post. His first task was to write an official letter to the King, and he took the opportunity to append a flattering epigram.

As James often came to hunt near Cambridge, Herbert soon had opportunities to gain his favour and exploited them successfully. His personal advantages were considerable, for he was of good family and breeding, handsome, learned and eloquent. He had powerful allies at Court also: his kinsman, the Earl of Pembroke, was Lord Chamberlain; his eldest brother, Edward (later Lord Herbert of Cherbury, a distinguished soldier, poet, philosopher and diplomat), had gained court favour and become Ambassador to France; and his younger brother, Henry, became Master of the Revels in 1623. After 1621, Herbert seems to have spent more time at the Court than at Cambridge. From a modern viewpoint his behaviour may seem sycophantic and timeserving. By the standards of his own time, however, he was doing what any young man of his connections and ability would do in seeking the patronage of the King. Nevertheless, it is apparent that his intention to enter the Church had given place to more worldly ambitions.

In 1625, however, before Herbert had obtained the advancement he sought, James died. Presumably Herbert could well have gained the favour of his successor; but for reasons which are not clear he did not do so, but abandoned Court-life.

He was thirty-two when, towards the end of 1625, he announced his decision to enter into holy orders. No doubt he was encouraged in this not only by his mother but by Donne, who was staying at the family's home at Chelsea at the time. In 1626 Herbert was ordained deacon, and instituted by proxy to the canonry and prebend of Leighton Ecclesia, near Huntingdon. This was a sinecure and did not involve parish work; and Herbert apparently never officiated at Leighton or even visited it.

It was usual to seek ordination as a priest one year after becoming a deacon, but Herbert did not do so. He appears to have suffered a period of doubt as to his worthiness to become a priest. Also his health was particularly poor at this period and he was threatened with consumption. For his health's sake he stayed for about a year with his brother Henry in Essex. During 1627 his mother died, and a few months later he resigned his Oratorship.

In 1628 he went to stay with his stepfather's elder brother, Lord Danby, at Dauntsey, near Chippenham in Wiltshire. Here he made up his mind to enter the priesthood and to marry. After a brief courtship he married Danby's cousin, Jane Danvers, on 5th March 1628/29; and in 1630 he became Rector of Bemerton, near Salisbury, and was ordained priest. This rectory was in the gift of his kinsman, the Earl of Pembroke; but as the King had promoted the outgoing rector it was for him to make the presentation. At Pembroke's request, Charles bestowed it 'most willingly to Mr. Herbert, if it be worth his acceptance'.

At this time it was most unusual for a man of Herbert's birth and education to become a country parson or even to take orders at all. Moreover, Bemerton was a small and obscure parish, and both its churches were in bad repair. Having at last made his decision and become a priest, however, Herbert devoted himself to his calling so completely that all who knew him loved and reverenced him. His own prose work, *A Priest to the Temple, or, the Country Parson*, shows with what devotion he regarded his responsibility, for it sets down his ideals and was written, as he said, as 'a mark to aim at'. His friend Nicholas Ferrar, who had established a religious community at Little Gidding, near Huntingdon, later described him as 'a companion to the primitive Saints and a pattern or more for the age he lived in', and Izaak Walton and Lord Herbert of Cherbury both testify to his reputation for sanctity. He celebrated divine service twice a day and ministered actively to the needs of his parishioners, however humble they were.

However, Herbert's ministry at Bemerton lasted only three years, for his health was failing. He died on Friday, 1st March 1633, in his fortieth year, meeting his end with serenity and with a prayer on his lips.

Herbert's poems are almost all included in a collection called *The Temple*. More than half the one hundred and sixty poems in this collection were written during the Bemerton years, during which time he also revised many of his earlier poems. Though some early poems written in Latin had been published, none of his English verse had appeared in print; but some must have circulated in manuscript, for he had a reputation as a poet during his lifetime. After his death the manuscript of *The Temple* was conveyed to Nicholas Ferrar, who arranged for its publication within a year. The book was immediately successful, and was acclaimed both for its poetic excellence and for the piety of its author.

POETRY

The range of Herbert's poetry is limited: he wrote only on religious themes, and nearly all his poems are comparatively short lyrics. Their quality, however, both in content and technique, invites the adjective 'great'.

In considering the content of the poems we must contemplate the character and endowments of the man and the course of his life. He was, we remember, of aristocratic birth and breeding, handsome and courtly, intellectually brilliant. He achieved swift success in university life, and sought further distinction at Court. Then he turned his back on all this and after long hesitation became a humble country parson, so completely dedicated that in three short years he gained the reputation of a saint. Clearly, such a man was of complex character and his development was accompanied by deep spiritual conflicts. These conflicts are expressed in many of his poems.

Herbert was not troubled by doctrinal doubts, for he accepted whole-heartedly the tenets of the Church of England; nor is there any mysticism in his poems. His own words, in his last message to Nicholas Ferrar, clearly describe their subject matter: 'a picture of the many spiritual Conflicts that have past betwixt God and my Soul, before I could submit mine to the will of Jesus my Master, in whose service I have now found perfect freedom.' He writes of the problem of resignation, and of his sense of unworthiness; he explores and analyses as subtly as Donne his own emotions, moods and motives; he is constantly concerned with the relationship between God and man, constantly striving towards the closer knowledge of God and of himself.

One aspect of Herbert's poems which is likely to strike the reader at once is that many of them are direct colloquies with God, expressed in a conversational tone of remarkable intimacy, which, however, is controlled with such tact that it never degenerates into sentimentality. The effect is completely natural because of Herbert's ability to suggest the speaking voice. This he does with an ease and range—from the courtly to the vigorously colloquial—that give his verse a dramatic quality which his fondness for dialogue and questions makes particularly noticeable.

To achieve an effect of speech in blank verse is comparatively easy; Herbert's achievement is the more remarkable because he used a very wide variety of metrical forms. No less than one hundred and sixteen of his poems are written in forms which he does not repeat. His technical skill and inventiveness are extraordinary. Moreover, as his editor G. H. Palmer remarks, he 'invents for each lyrical situation exactly the rhythmic setting that befits it'. He writes with great economy, being adept at packing meaning into a small compass; and he is notably a poet of complete poems—that is to say that his poems make their effect as wholes, not as collections of brilliant fragments; and individual stanzas, lines and phrases suffer by being removed from their contexts.

Herbert's poetry expresses the combination of intellect and sensibility and the flexibility of attitude characteristic of Metaphysical wit; but his use of imagery and the conceit differs considerably from that of Donne. He does not draw his images from scientific or scholastic learning, as Donne often does, but from familiar everyday sources. Like Donne, he often surprises the reader into a new understanding; but he does this not by outlandish comparisons, but by the contrast between the dignity of his subject matter and the familiarity of the image used to illustrate it, as in *Affliction*:

At first thou gav'st me milk and sweetnesses . . .

Despite the intellectual vigour and the subtlety of Herbert's poems, they are always graceful and usually lucid. Moreover, they are expressed in language of a purity which drew from Coleridge the comment: 'nothing can be more fine, manly and unaffected.'

NOTES ON THE POEMS OF GEORGE HERBERT

32. AFFLICTION

In this poem Herbert surveys the course of his life, seeing in its vicissitudes the hand of God leading him to the priesthood. Doubtful whether he can sustain the burden thrust upon him, he threatens to abandon God's service, and concludes with a paradoxical appeal.

l.13. 'What pleasures could I lack when I served the king of pleasures?'

l.25. 'My flesh began to speak in pain to my soul as follows . . .' (the next three lines are what the flesh said).

l.32. *my friends die:* perhaps refers to the deaths of the Duke of Richmond and the Marquis of Hamilton, two of Herbert's most influential patrons at Court; of King James; of Lord Bacon; and of his mother. All these deaths occurred during the period 1624–27.

l.38. A secular career, presumably at the Court or as a Secretary of State, the appointment that Herbert hoped for.

l.47. *where:* 'to the point, or state of mind, at which . . .'

l.53. *crosse-bias me:* 'give me an inclination other than my own' (Grierson, *Metaphysical Lyrics and Poems*, p. 230). The metaphor is from the game of bowls.

ll.65–6. 'Though it may mean that you cast me out entirely from your mind, if I cannot love you entirely and without reservation (because of the trials you impose upon me) let me be released from loving you at all.' This is, of course, a paradoxical assertion of the impossibility of quitting God's service, and at the same time a protest at the pain that his feelings of inadequacy and unworthiness cause to him.

34. THE PEARL. Matth. xiii. 45

In this poem, Herbert surveys what he has renounced in order to devote himself to God, making it clear that the renunciation is deliberate and made with full awareness of the value of what he is giving up.

Matth. xiii. 45: 'Again, the kingdom of heaven is like unto a merchant man, seeking goodly pearls.'

ll.1–2. *the head and pipes that feed the presse:* this is difficult. It may be an allusion to Zech. iv. 12, to the two olive branches which through two golden pipes empty the golden oil out of themselves to feed the bowl for the seven lamps. Or it may be a complex image referring to an olive or wine press, but involving also, by a pun on *presse*, a printing press, by which knowledge is disseminated. Canon Hutchinson suggests that *the head* is the universities, the fountain of knowledge, and the *pipes* are those who mediate that knowledge to the world in the learned professions. A simpler way of putting it might be that the universities are *the head* and scholars who write books in order to disseminate knowledge gained there are the *pipes*.

l.5.   conspire: plot together; perhaps a reference to astrology.

l.8.   stock and surplus: perhaps 'the learning we inherit, and that which we add to it' (H. C. Beeching, *Lyra Sacra*).

ll.13–17. 'I know how to gauge by the rules of courtesy who wins in a contest of doing favours; when each party is urged by ambition to do all he can by look or deed to win the world and bind it on his back.'

l.32.   not sealed, but with open eyes: 'not in blind ignorance, but fully aware of what I am doing'.

ll.33–40. 'I understand the conditions of sale, and the price I must pay, but, after all, it is thy guidance rather than my intelligence that brings me to thee' (Hutchinson).

l.38.   silk twist: a silken cord.

36.   PRAYER

This sonnet is a sort of meditative catalogue of conceits, but notice the simple phrase with which it ends.

l.1.   Angels age: Canon Hutchinson suggests the meaning 'prayer acquaints man with the blessed timeless existence of the angels'. The phrase is contrasted with 'Man's age'—threescore and ten.

l.5.   Engine: a missile. In another poem, Herbert refers to prayer as artillery.

l.7. According to Genesis, the Creation took six days. *Transposing* means 'altering' or 'affecting'.

l.10.   Exalted Manna: Manna which rises to Heaven instead of falling from it.

36.   REDEMPTION

Another example of Herbert's skill in handling the sonnet. Note the 'parable' form.

37.   EASTER

Easter is actually a poem of six stanzas, but falls into two parts, of which I print the second. The first three stanzas are metrically different from these three.

l.6. 'Though he gives light and the East gives perfume.'

l.11.   three hundred: Herbert is taking a poetic liberty with the number of days in a year.

38. EASTER WINGS

This is an example of metrical ingenuity, but the ingenuity extends beyond making a pattern. '. . . the diminuendo and crescendo that bring [the shape of the wings on the page] about are expressive both of the rise and fall of the lark's song and flight (Herbert's image) and also of the fall of man and his resurrection in Christ (the subject that the image represents).' (Joan Bennett, *Four Metaphysical Poets*, 1934, p. 66.)

l.10.   Adam's fall was thought by some theologians to have occasioned the Redemption.

l.19.   *imp*: a term from falconry, meaning to strengthen or restore strength to a wing by engrafting feathers in it.

38. JORDAN

In this poem, Herbert affirms his intention of devoting his poetic talents to truth (i.e. the service of religion), and not to the themes, such as profane love, which preoccupied most of his contemporaries. He expresses contempt for the pastoral allegorical poetry of imitators of Spenser.

The title has provoked various explanations. The simplest seems to be that the waters of Jordan purify, and Herbert proposes to write poetry that is free from the impurities of 'fictions and false hair', etc.

l.6.   *except*: unless.

l.7.   *sudden*: unexpected.

l.12.   *Riddle who list, for me . . .*: let anyone concoct riddles who wants to, for all I care . . .

   pull for Prime: refers to primero, a card-game which was the original of poker. The expression means 'to draw for a card or cards which will make the player *prime*' (O.E.D.).

39. THE CHURCH WINDOWS

Herbert wrote a number of poems in which some part of the building or furniture of a church is used to illustrate a theme.

l.2.   *crazie*: flawed or cracked.

l.6.   *anneal*: to fix colours in glass by heating it after it has been painted.

40. VERTUE

l.5.   *angrie*: an angry face is red.

l.11.   *closes*: a musical term, referring to the cadences or conclusions of musical phrases or movements.

l.15.   *coal*: the conflagration at the end of the world would turn all except virtue to 'coal' (i.e. cinders).

40. LIFE

ll.2–3. These lines are what he said to himself when he made the posy.

l.15. Flowers, like herbs, were thought to have medicinal properties.

41. EMPLOYMENT

l.1. Note the abruptly vigorous opening.

l.2. would: wishes to.

l.4. Quitting: leaving.

l.5. complexions: constitutions. According to the mediaeval conception, which was still accepted by many, everything in the universe was composed of different combinations of the four elements, fire, air, water and earth. Man, who was himself thought of as a microcosm or 'little world', was similarly composed, the elements in him appearing in the form of four 'humours' or bodily fluids. These were: (i) choler, or yellow bile, which corresponded to fire and embodied the qualities of heat and dryness; (ii) blood, corresponding to air (hot and moist); (iii) phlegm, corresponding to water (cold and moist); (iv) black bile, corresponding to earth (cold and dry). One's physical and mental type depended on which of these 'humours' predominated. As the later image of 'earth' makes clear, a 'cold complexion' would be one in which 'black bile' predominated.

l.6. a quick coal: a piece of carbon glowing without flame (O.E.D.). This is in contrast to a dead 'coal' (cinder) as in *Vertue.*

l.11. elements: as explained in note to *l.5.*

l.14. earth: was the lowest of the elements because it was the least active. So he who remains inactive, who 'lets his own ashes choke his soul', is the basest of men.

l.18. still: always.

l.22. busie: because it bore fruit and blossom both at the same time.

l.26. still: always.

ll.26–28. Herbert means that as an excuse for our laziness we delude ourselves that we are too young or too old—at any rate, never ready. Thus we let our opportunities to *unfold our wares* slip.

42. THE COLLAR

This magnificent poem is remarkable for its dramatic quality and its passionate force. Notice how the movement communicates the rebellious mood and its eventual subsidence.

The collar is a symbol of discipline, and the point of the title is that the poem deals with the desire to 'slip one's neck out of the collar' of God's service.

l.6. in suit: 'Herbert compares the waiter on God's will to the suitor at Court'(Grierson).

l.14. *bayes:* laurel crown.

l.16. *wasted:* laid waste.

l.29. *deaths head:* a skull was a *memento mori* (L. 'remember you must die'), or emblem of mortality.

43. THE PULLEY

This poem recalls the story of Pandora's box.

The pulley: the restlessness of man is a pulley intended to draw him up to God.

l.15. *both:* both God and man.

ll.16–17. *rest . . . restlessnesse:* a play on words; *rest* here means 'remainder'. Such ambiguities keep the reader alert.

44. THE FLOWER

One of the most beautiful of Herbert's poems.

ll.2–4. *Ev'n . . . bring:* rather obscure, the more so as *demean* can mean 'bearing' (cf. 'demeanour') or 'demesne' (estate, territory one possesses). Canon Hutchinson gives the general sense as: 'The spring flowers not only have their own intrinsic beauty, but they are also welcome as a sign of the passing of winter; so are the returns of grace the more welcome after a time of spiritual aridity'.

l.16. *quickning:* restoring life to.

l.18. The *passing-bell* is tolled at the hour of a person's death, slowly and on a single note. Chiming bells produce a cheerful and varied sound.

ll.19–20. We are wrong to say a thing *is* (i.e. exists in itself, or unchangeably); 'it is what it is by God's immediate ordinance' (H. C. Beeching).

l.25. *Off'ring:* aiming.

ll.32–35. Compared to the *frost* of God's least frown, the Arctic and Antarctic poles are zones 'where all things burn'.

l.44. *glide:* gently and imperceptibly die away.

l.45. 'When once we are able to discover and experience the truth of this . . .'

46. AARON

See Exodus xxviii. In order to carry out his priestly function and bring peace to his people, Aaron had to wear the divinely prescribed regalia; for the same purpose, Herbert must be 'drest' in perfect submission to God.

Sir Herbert Grierson points out that 'Each verse of Herbert's poem suggests metrically the swelling and dying sound of a bell; and, like a bell, the rhymes reiterate the same sound.'

l.1. Aaron had to wear a mitre bearing a gold plate engraved with the words 'Holiness to the Lord'.

l.2.   He had to wear also a breastplate, into which he was instructed to put 'the Urim and the Thummim'. These were oracular stones. *Urim* is the plural of the Hebrew word *ur*, meaning 'light'; and *tummim* (thummim) of *tom*, meaning 'perfection'.

l.3.   *Harmonious bells:* about the hem of his robe Aaron wore bells and pomegranates.

l.8.   *A noise:* may mean 'a band of musicians' here.

l.18.   *striking:* a pun. Besides the obvious sense, *striking* refers to the action of the clapper striking a bell.

47. LOVE

This poem is a sort of dramatized parable, thus combining two of Herbert's favourite forms. Herbert characteristically stresses God's loving kindness.

THOMAS CAREW

LIFE

Thomas Carew (pron. 'Carey') was born between June 1594 and June 1595, probably at West Wickham, in Kent, where his parents lived at the time. He came of good family. His father, Matthew, was descended from a landed Cornish family; and his mother, Alice, was the daughter of Sir John Ryvers, once Lord Mayor of London. Matthew Carew was a Doctor of Civil Law and a Master in Chancery, and was knighted in 1603.

About 1598 the family went to live in London, in Chancery Lane. Nothing is known of Thomas's boyhood and early education. In June 1608, at the age of thirteen, he matriculated at Merton College, Oxford, the Warden of which, Henry Savile, was a kinsman by marriage. Carew took his B.A. on 31st January 1610/11, and in 1612 he was incorporated a B.A. of Cambridge. It was intended that he should follow his father's profession, the law; and he was admitted to the Middle Temple in August 1612.

By February 1613, however, Sir Matthew was complaining, in a letter to a friend, that Thomas was neglecting his studies. At the same time, Sir Matthew suffered very serious financial losses. Presumably because of both these factors, Thomas left the Middle Temple in order to become secretary to his relative by marriage, Sir Dudley Carleton, English Ambassador at Venice.

Carew appears to have spent about eighteen months in Italy, during which time he became acquainted with Italian literature and learnt languages. Carleton, and presumably Carew, returned to London in December 1615. In 1616 Carleton went as Ambassador to the Hague, and

Carew again accompanied him. Carleton was apparently well satisfied with his secretary's services. After some months, however, Carew fell into disgrace. He had committed to paper 'for his private ends and direction' (as he said later) some aspersions on the characters of Sir Dudley and Lady Carleton; and Sir Dudley found the document. Without revealing his discovery, Carleton sent Carew back to England, much to the bewilderment of Sir Matthew. Two months later, Carleton informed Sir Matthew of the reasons for his son's dismissal. The old man was bitterly angry, the more so because Thomas, on being taxed with the matter, appeared unrepentant. Thomas had meanwhile attempted to find employment in the service of several other noblemen, but without success. In December, his father complained in a letter that his son 'haueng geuen over al studye here eyther of lawe or other lerning, vagrantly and debauchedlye takethe no maner of good but al lewde courses, with the which he will weary me and al his other friendes, and run hym self into utter ruyn'.

It should, perhaps, be observed that Sir Matthew was an old man when Thomas was born, and his attitude towards his son was probably embittered by senility and by his financial misfortunes. Nevertheless, Thomas was obviously far from being an ideal son. Despite his own lack of employment and his father's continual money troubles, he seems to have spent the next two or three years enjoying himself or, as his father put it, 'myspending his tyme'. He must have been often at the Court at Whitehall, and he is mentioned as being one of two 'squires of high degree for cost and bravery' present at the creation of Prince Charles as Prince of Wales. His poems to Celia presumably relate to a love affair, or perhaps more than one, of this period.

On 2nd August 1618 Sir Matthew died, aged eighty-five. His house in Chancery Lane was sold, and his elder son, also Sir Matthew (he had been knighted in 1611) moved to an estate in Worcestershire, where his mother joined him.

On 13th May 1619, Carew accompanied Sir Edward Herbert (George Herbert's brother, later Lord Herbert of Cherbury) on his embassy to Paris. Herbert, writing of his retinue, refers to 'Thomas Carew, that excellent wit'. While in Paris Carew became familiar with French poetry, and may have met the Italian poet Marino, then resident there, whose lyrics influenced him considerably.

We do not know how long Carew remained in France or how he supported himself on his return to England. He probably returned about 1621. Back in England he became the associate of many of the most brilliant figures of the time. He was one of the group of friends and admirers of Ben Jonson known as 'the tribe of Ben', and his friends included Sir John Suckling, William Davenant, Aurelian Townshend and George Sandys. There is no evidence that he ever met John Donne, but he apparently heard him preach and certainly read his poems with care. His talent and wit brought him not only the friendship of other poets, but also popularity at Court. Clarendon, writing of the period after 1625, when Charles I had come to the throne, briefly describes Carew, in his *Life*: '. . . He was very much esteemed by the most eminent persons in the Court, and well looked upon by the King . . . He was a Person of a pleasant and facetious Wit, and made many Poems (especially in the amorous Way) which for the Sharpness of the Fancy and the Elegancy of the Language . . . were at least equal, if not superior to any of that Time.' Only ten of Carew's poems appeared in print during his lifetime, and his popularity as a poet was based on circulation of manuscripts. A large number of manuscript copies of his poems were made.

Despite Court favour and the friendship of influential people such as the Earl of Anglesey, the Duke of Buckingham's younger brother, it was not until 1630 that Carew received an official appointment at Court. He then became a Gentleman of the Privy Chamber Extraordinary, and Sewer in Ordinary to the King.

From this time onwards Carew seems to have led the sort of life his pleasure-loving temperament craved. His charm, his quick wit and his serviceability kept him in Court favour and out of debt. In 1634 his masque, *Coelum Britannicum*, with settings by Inigo Jones, was performed on Shrove Tuesday at Whitehall by the King and his gentlemen. His reputation as a poet was high, and his notoriety as a rake seems also to have been considerable (Izaak Walton refers to him as 'a poet of note and a great libertine in his life and talk'). As might be expected, he took little interest in the political and religious controversies of the day. His attitude towards public affairs is perhaps best indicated by his poem *In answer of an Elegiacall Letter upon the death of the King of Sweden* (Gustavus Adolphus) *from* Aurelian Townsend, *inviting me to write on that subject:*

> Tourneyes, Masques, Theaters, better become
> Our *Halcyon* dayes; what though the German Drum
> Bellow for freedom and revenge, the noise
> Concernes not us, nor should divert our joyes.

He seems, however, to have had some fits of remorse about the licentiousness of his life. Walton records that during a 'dangerose fit of sickness' he sent for a clergyman, John Hales, 'and desyrd his aduise and absolution wch mr Hales vppon a promise of amendment gaue him (this was I think in the country) but mr cary came to london fell to his old company and into a more visable Scandalus life . . .' Walton goes on to record that in Carew's last illness he again 'procur'd mr Ha to come to him in this his sicknes and agony of minde desyring earnestly after a confession of many of his sins to have his prayers and his absolution. mr Ha, told him he shood have his prayers, but wood by noe meanes giue him then ether the sacrament or absolution.' It appears, therefore, that Carew's periods of concern for his spiritual state coincided with periods of dangerous illness (possibly the effects of venereal disease). However this may be, there is no doubt about the reverence and sense of sin expressed in his fine poem *To my worthy friend Mr. George Sandys*, written in 1638.

In 1639 he took part in the King's expedition against Scotland in the first Bishops' War, and suffered considerable hardships. This experience perhaps aggravated his ill-health, for about 21st March 1639/40 he died, aged about forty-four. Clarendon records that 'his Glory was that after fifty Years of his Life, spent with less Severity in Exactness than it ought to have been, He died with the greatest Remorse for that Licence, and with the greatest Manifestation of Christianity, that his best Friends could desire'. According to another writer, Anthony à Wood, King Charles 'always esteemed him to the last one of the most celebrated wits in his court, and therefore by him as highly valued, so afterwards grieved at his untimely death'.

Carew was buried beside his father in St. Anne's Chapel, St. Dunstan's-in-the-West, but there is now no trace there of his tomb.

POETRY

Carew was the leading member of a group of poets known as the Cavalier Poets, all of whom were associated, to a greater or less extent, with the Court of Charles I. Other members of the group included Suckling, Lovelace, and Herrick. Carew was one of the most popular poets of his time, as is shown by numerous tributes to him by fellow poets and other writers. He was not a major poet: his virtues are representative of a particular phase of culture; but, as Dr. F. R. Leavis has said, 'He has individual force enough to be representative with unusual vitality'.

Like that of his greater successor, Marvell, Carew's poetry combines the influences of Donne and Jonson, and he was fully aware of his debt. His *Elegie upon the Death of the Deane of Pauls, Dr. John Donne* is not only a fine poem but a remarkable demonstration of critical insight; and his poem *To Ben Jonson* records the awareness of the value of careful artistry which the Cavaliers learnt from him:

> Thy labour'd workes shall live, when Time devoures
> Th' abortive offspring of [others'] hastie houres.

Carew had neither the intellectual range and profundity nor the intensity of passion of Donne, and he does not use Donne's dramatically forceful broken rhythms. Though he praises Donne in the *Elegie* for doing away with the classical impedimenta—

> the goodly exil'd traine
> Of gods and goddesses, which in thy just raigne
> Were banish'd nobler Poems

—his own work is strewn with classical references. His debt to Donne is to be found in his habit of critical awareness which expresses itself in analysis of feelings and flexibility of attitude; his ability to sustain and elaborate poetic arguments; his vivid phrases and conceits (sometimes actually borrowed from Donne); and, sometimes, his achievement of that fusion of feeling, thought and image which is characteristic of Donne.

Jonson's influence manifests itself in Carew's poetry in two ways: in his form and style, and in his themes. Like Jonson, Carew is a careful and conscious artist. His work is characterized by a remarkable sense of form and structure, by lucidity and conciseness, and control of feeling which expresses itself in a polished urbanity of tone and attitude. He writes in an idiom which combines courtly sophistication with racy colloquialism. His themes, like Jonson's, are often drawn from Catullus and other Classical lyrists. They are conventional, but he handles them with vitality and conviction because the conventions are entirely congenial: they correspond to the attitudes to experience, particularly of human relationships, which he and the other poets of the Court held.

Though Carew was a rake and a frivolous courtier, it must not be assumed that his work is superficial and merely charming. His *Elegie* on Donne and his poem *To my worthy friend Mr. George Sandys* clearly show his intelligence and his depth. *Ingratefull beauty threatned* may look at first glance no more than a conventional lyric, but closer examination will reveal that its graceful poise is accompanied by considerable strength: that it reveals civilized intelligence and maturity. The elegy on *Maria Wentworth* reveals characteristic Metaphysical wit in its combination of lightness with seriousness:

So though a Virgin, yet a Bride
To every Grace, she justifi'd
A chaste Poligamie, and dy'd.

The fourth and fifth stanzas of this poem, incidentally, illustrate an important aspect of the poetry of Carew and the other Caroline poets: that it points forward to the Augustan mode, and particularly to Pope.

Nevertheless, the Caroline school of which Carew is the leading representative must not be thought of as a mere transitional stage towards Augustanism. Their poetry was the expression of a culture which no longer existed after the Restoration. 'It represents', as F. R. Leavis has said, 'a Court culture . . . that preserved, in its sophisticated way, an element of the tradition of chivalry, and that had turned the studious or naïvely enthusiastic Renaissance classicizing and poetizing of an earlier period into something intimately bound up with contemporary life and manners—something consciously both mature and, while contemporary, traditional.' No true Court culture has existed since.

NOTES ON THE POEMS OF THOMAS CAREW

48. SONG: MEDIOCRITIE IN LOVE REJECTED

The theme of this poem has been handled by many poets, but Carew's treatment of it gives it renewed vitality. The movement suggests song and yet is clearly related to speech. The diction is characteristically direct; the logical development derives from both Donne and Jonson; the imagery of the first stanza, with its geographical reference, is typically Metaphysical.

l.8. Danaë: the mother of Perseus. Her father confined her in a brazen tower, but Zeus visited and seduced her there in the form of a shower of gold.

l.11. My Vulture-hopes: his hopes, while unrealized, torture him. If they are not gratified, it is best that they should be swept away completely. The image is drawn from the story of Prometheus: Zeus punished him for stealing fire from Heaven and giving it to mankind, by chaining him to a rock and sending a vulture to feed on his liver every day.

48. TO MY INCONSTANT MISTRIS

The theme had been used by both Catullus and Propertius. The tone is a blend of seriousness and irony. The religious conceit is typically Metaphysical.

49. A DEPOSITION FROM LOVE

A fine example of Carew's sense of structure: the shapely stanzas combine in the perfect unity of the whole.

50. INGRATEFULL BEAUTY THREATNED

A brilliant combination of Metaphysical imagery and Jonsonian grace.

*l.*6. *impt:* see note to Herbert's *Easter Wings*, *l.*19.

*ll.*7–8. in talking of the *killing power* of Celia's voice and eyes, Carew may have had in mind the voices of the Sirens and the eyes of the Basilisk or the Gorgons, though the associations of the last two are unsuitable.

51. TO SAXHAM

Little Saxham, in Suffolk, was the home of Carew's friends, the Crofts family. He probably stayed there frequently. This poem is modelled on Jonson's *Penshurst*. It reminds us that in Charles I's time the Court was still closely in touch with the great country houses and the social responsibilities associated with them.

*l.*11. *sterv'd:* caused to die.

*l.*12. *Much poore:* many of the poor.

*l.*18. 'had been your aviary exclusively'.

*l.*42. *Hind:* servant.

53. THE INSCRIPTION ON THE TOMBE OF THE LADY MARY WENTWORTH

Maria Wentworth died in January 1632, aged eighteen, and was buried at St. George's Church, Toddington, Bedfordshire, where her tomb, inscribed with the first six stanzas of Carew's poem, is still to be seen. She was the second daughter of the Earl of Cleveland, and her mother was the sister of Carew's friend, John Crofts.

*ll.*4–6. This conceit is borrowed from Donne, *The Second Anniversarie*, *ll.*183–184:

> . . . This to thy Soule allow,
> Thinke thy shell broke, thinke thy Soule hatch'd but now.

54. AN ELEGIE UPON THE DEATH OF THE DEANE OF PAULS, DR. JOHN DONNE

Donne died on 31st March 1631. This poem was printed among the *Elegies upon the Author* in Donne's Poems, 1633, but was written considerably before that date. Not only the content but also the style make Carew's debt to and admiration for Donne abundantly clear.

The opening lines suggest that the poem was written before any other elegies to Donne had appeared.

*l.*4. *dowe-bak't:* dough-baked, i.e. not perfectly baked, and therefore imperfect, tasteless, flat.

*l.*5. *uncisor'd:* unscissored; with carelessly barbered or uncut hair.

*l.*22. *Delphique:* Delphi was the seat of the principal temple of Apollo, the god of music and poetry.

*l.*23. *Promethean:* see note to *Mediocritie in Love Rejected, l.*11. The suggestion of *ll.*21–24 is that Donne was the inspiration of contemporary poetry, and that inspiration has died with him.

*ll.*25–33. Carew refers to Donne's revolt against the imitativeness of his predecessors and contemporaries.

*l.*64. *Of gods and goddesses:* a reference to the fashion of ornamenting poetry with references to classical mythology.

*l.*66. *th'Metamorphoses:* Donne's predecessors had drawn largely on Ovid's *Metamorphoses.*

*l.*87. *I will not draw the envy:* Carew appears to mean that he will not incur the envy of other poets by attempting a catalogue of all Donne's virtues; he will leave part of this privilege to others.

57. TO A LADY THAT DESIRED I WOULD LOVE HER

It has been suggested, on stylistic grounds, that this poem might be by Lord Herbert of Cherbury, but the evidence for such a view is unconvincing. The poem was printed in the 1640 edition of Carew's poems.

*l.*13. *Loves curst Rebels:* those who refuse to accept the sway of Love, and so compel their admirers to celebrate them in poems lamenting unrequited love.

58. TO MY WORTHY FRIEND MR. GEORGE SANDYS

This appeared with other commendatory poems in the second (1638) edition of Sandys' *A Paraphrase upon the Divine Poems,* a translation of the Psalms.

*l.*14. cf. David dancing before the ark of God (2 Samuel vi. 13–14).

*l.*28. *the first Faire:* God.

59. A SONG: ASK ME NO MORE

*ll.*3–4. Mr. Rhodes Dunlap explains this by reference to Aristotle's account of the four causes: the material, the formal, the efficient, and the purposive. The concept of the formal cause (as the relation 2:1 in the octave) applies here: 'in the lady's beauty Carew sees the very essence or idea of roses'.

*l.*11. *dividing:* descanting or warbling.

*l.*18. *The Phenix:* the phoenix was a fabulous Arabian bird. It was said to live for five hundred years, and then to make a nest of spices and burn itself to ashes from which it was then reborn to live another five hundred years.

RICHARD CRASHAW

Richard Crashaw was born late in 1612 or early in 1613. He was the son of the Rev. William Crashaw and his first wife. The latter died during the poet's infancy. William Crashaw, at the time of his son's birth, was preacher at the Temple Church in London, and later rector of White-chapel. He was a Puritan, noted for his zeal in anti-papal polemic. He was also an ardent collector of books, and his library contained much Roman Catholic literature (collected largely for the purpose of exploring its errors), which may have contributed to his son's subsequent interest in Catholicism.

William Crashaw died in 1626, when Richard was about fourteen. The boy apparently came under the guardianship of two lawyers, and entered the Charterhouse in 1629. In 1631 he was sent as an exhibitioner to Pembroke College, Cambridge.

During his early years at Cambridge, Crashaw wrote English and Latin verse of an occasional nature, and in 1634, the year of his graduation as B.A., he published a volume of Latin epigrams. By this date he had already come under High Anglican influence, both his tutor and the Master of Pembroke being High Churchmen. In 1635, Crashaw was elected a Fellow of Peterhouse, the centre of High Churchmanship at Cambridge; and for the next eight years this college was his home. Though there is no record of Crashaw's entry into holy orders, he must have become a priest by 1639, for he was then curate of the church of Little St. Mary's (which had close connections with Peterhouse) and he also held office as the college catechist.

Crashaw's life during his fellowship seems to have suited his temperament ideally. He was able to spend much time in reading and writing, and also in exercising his talents for drawing, painting, engraving and music. Much of his writing was concerned with translation, and he became proficient in Italian and Spanish, in addition to the classical languages. Thus he came to be influenced by the writings of St. Teresa (the Spanish mystic, whose canonization in 1622 resulted in wide circulation of her books and much writing about her), and by Italian poets of the Counter-Reformation—particularly Marino, whose extravagance of hyperbole and sensuous sweetness of style had a marked effect on Crashaw's own poetry. In addition to his artistic and intellectual leanings, however, Crashaw had the instincts of an ascetic and a recluse. He was quite indifferent to worldly and material matters—even to food and drink; and so he lived an almost monastic life. He frequently spent nights of prayer and vigil in Little St. Mary's, and is said to have composed his poems there. Apparently, he also sometimes went 'into retreat' at Nicholas Ferrar's religious community at Little Gidding.

This serene existence, however, was disrupted by the Civil War. In 1643, Cromwell's forces occupied Cambridge, and Peterhouse, as a centre of what the Parliamentary Commissioners regarded as Papistry (the college had, moreover, contributed financially to the King's cause) suffered accordingly. Crashaw was ejected from his fellowship in 1644, but had already left Cambridge.

We next hear of him in Leyden, and then it seems probable that he returned to England for a while, possibly going to Oxford, since the King's Court was there. Next we hear of him in Paris, and by this time he had become a Roman Catholic. Abraham Cowley, who had been an intimate friend of Crashaw's at Cambridge, found him there in a state of destitution, helped him, and brought him to the notice of the Queen, Henrietta Maria, whose Court was then in Paris. She provided him with letters of introduction, and he set out for Rome.

In Rome, Crashaw eventually became secretary to Cardinal Pallotto, an estimable and pious man. Crashaw admired him, but found that the morals of the Cardinal's retinue were extremely lax. He reported this to his master. Pallotto, fearing that Crashaw's fellow attendants might revenge themselves on him for his exposure of them, decided that he was not safe in Rome and appointed him to a minor post at the church of Our Lady of Loretto. Loretto was one of the most sacred shrines in Christendom. It contained a tiny stone house in which the Virgin Mary was said to have been born (the house was supposed to have been transported by angels from Palestine), and several other legends were attached to it. There can be little doubt that Crashaw, an ardent devotee of the Virgin, was blissfully happy there. His service, however, was fated to be short; he was inducted in April 1649, and on 21st August he died of a fever. Cowley, an Anglican, comments, in his elegy on Crashaw:

> How well (blest Swan) did Fate contrive thy death;
> And made thee render up thy tuneful breath
> In thy great *Mistress* Arms? thou most divine
> And richest *Off'ering* of *Loretto's Shrine*!

POETRY

The main body of Crashaw's poetry appeared in *Steps to the Temple* (1646), a collection of religious poems to which a section of secular poems, *The Delights of the Muses*, was attached. The title *Steps to the Temple* recalls Herbert, but Crashaw was utterly unlike Herbert as a poet.

Though Crashaw's work is clearly related to the Metaphysical tradition, it diverges very considerably from it, being greatly influenced by Italian poetry, as I have mentioned earlier. Whereas in the poetry of Donne and Herbert the conceit functions as an integral part of a poem, Crashaw's use of it is largely ornamental. Crashaw lacks the intellectual range and power of Donne, and the restraint and artistry of Herbert. His later, religious poetry is chiefly remarkable for its outbursts of passionate, lyrical intensity. It expresses no painful self-analysis such as we find in Donne and Herbert, but ardent adoration and joy, for acceptance of the Roman faith entirely satisfied Crashaw and left no room for doubt or uneasiness of spirit. His feeling is expressed in verse of great sensuousness; and we find the poet whose secular 'love poems' were of an essentially idealistic nature, unrelated to any real amorous experience, frequently using the language of erotic poetry to express religious emotion.

Crashaw is an uneven poet, lacking in discipline and critical sensibility. There are times when his conceits are impossibly extravagant, and when his sensuous sweetness becomes cloying. At his best, however, his passionate eloquence is extremely impressive, and his work has, as Sir Herbert Grierson observed, 'two of the supreme qualities of great lyric poetry . . . ardour and music'.

NOTES ON THE POEMS OF RICHARD CRASHAW

61. LOVES HOROSCOPE

This is one of the poems in which Crashaw comes nearest to Donne. It is one of the best of his secular pieces; but, having no basis in lived experience, it lacks the ardour of his religious verse.

l.13. revolutions: an astrological image.

l.25. twin'd upon: were united on.

63. THE HYMN OF SAINT THOMAS IN ADORATION OF THE BLESSED SACRAMENT

The absence of doubt or spiritual conflict, the complete and untroubled surrender to faith, and the sensuous delight in the sacrament make this eloquent poem typical of Crashaw.

l.9. Your ports: the 'doors' of the senses.

l.18.   *the faithfull thiefe:* one of the malefactors who were crucified with Christ (*v.* Luke xxiii. 39–43).

l.21.   *than:* then.

ll.21–24.   *v.* John xx. 24–28.

l.26.   The body and blood of Christ which concealed his divinity are in turn concealed in the sacramental bread and wine.

l.41.   *gust:* taste.

l.45.   the pelican was thought to wound her own breast in order to feed her young with her blood.

65.   A HYMN TO THE NAME AND HONOR OF THE ADMIRABLE SAINT TERESA

St. Teresa (1515–82), the Spanish mystic, famous for her visions, belonged to the Carmelite order, of which she was an energetic reformer. Her writings greatly affected Crashaw even before he became a Roman Catholic. This impassioned celebration of her spiritual martyrdom is perhaps his finest poem. It has more intellectual strength and less extravagance and cloying lushness than most of his work. Notice particularly the dramatic vigour of the opening.

l.32.   *nonage:* period of immaturity; state of being under age.

l.71.   *race:* tear.

l.78.   *funerall:* death (*v. l*.110).

ll.79–80.   Crashaw refers, here and later in the poem, to an incident recorded in St. Teresa's autobiographical work, translated into English in 1642 under the title of *The Flaming Hart.* St. Teresa recounts a vision of an angel, who 'had a long Dart of gold in his hand; and at the end of the iron below, me thought, there was a little fire; and I conceaued, that he thrust it, after such a manner, as that it passed the verie inwards, of my Bowells; and when he drew it back, me thought, it carried away, as much, as it had touched within me; and left all that, which remained, wholy inflamed with a great love of Almightye God. The pain of it, was so excessive, that it forced me to utter those groanes; and the suavitie, which that extremitie of paine gave, was also so very excessive, that there was no desiring at all, to be ridd of it; nor can the Soule then, receaue anie contentment at all, in lesse, then God Almightie himself.'

ll.123–124.   *The Moon of maiden stars, thy white Mistresse:* the Virgin Mary. The imagery of whiteness refers not only to purity and virginity, but also to the whiteness of the robes of the Carmelite order.

l.143.   *thy spouse:* as a nun, Teresa was the bride of Christ.

l.175.   *score:* account.

HENRY VAUGHAN

Henry Vaughan was the elder of twin brothers, born in 1621 to Thomas and Denise Vaughan of Trenewydd, or Newton (its English name), a small estate in the parish of Llansantffraed, Breconshire. He was of wholly Welsh extraction, and was in the habit of calling himself 'Silurist' after the 'Silures', the local British tribe in Roman times. The Newton estate was small, but the family was of aristocratic descent and connections. Though Vaughan never claimed kinship with George Herbert, whose work influenced him greatly, the Herberts and Vaughans were connected through a common ancestor, Dafydd ap Llewellen, known as David Gam. This famous warrior had died at Agincourt, and was the 'Davy Gam, esquire' mentioned in the list of casualties read in Shakespeare's *Henry V*.

Newton was about five miles from the River Usk, and the countryside is of impressive beauty. The fact that Vaughan spent most of his life there is important, for one of the most distinctive features of his poetry is the loving observation of nature embodied in it.

After receiving their early education from a local clergyman, both boys, it seems, went to Jesus College, Oxford. I say 'it seems', because there is no convincing record of Henry's membership of the college. However, it appears probable that he was at Oxford for two years from 1638 to 1640, before going to London, where he resided for two years, to study law. Probably Vaughan's father did not intend that Henry should make the law his profession, but rather that he should acquire a general knowledge of it, which would be useful to him when he inherited the estate (for, as the elder twin, he was his father's heir). At any rate, there is no record of Vaughan's admission to any of the Inns of Court, and he was never called to the Bar. His early poems show that his interest during his stay was mainly in literary society and the political events of the time. At the outbreak of war in 1642 he returned to Wales.

After his return, according to Aubrey, 'he was a clarke sometime to Judge Sir Marmaduke Lloyd', who was Chief Justice of the Brecon circuit and, as Vaughan himself was, an ardent Royalist and supporter of the Church. In 1645, Lloyd was taken prisoner at Hereford by the Parliamentary forces, and dismissed from his office. How long Vaughan served him, and in what precise capacity, we do not know. From allusions in Vaughan's poems, it seems that he was at some time engaged in military service for the Royalist cause; but this also is uncertain, and we cannot say whether he actually bore arms.

In 1646 Vaughan married Catherine Wise, of Coleshill, Warwickshire, and settled at Newton on his father's estate (the latter lived on until 1658). In this year also, Vaughan's first book, *Poems, With the tenth Satyre of Iuvenal Englished*, was published. These were secular poems, modelled on the work of various poets he admired, including Donne and William Habington, with such titles as *Les Amours* and *To Amoret, Walking in a Stormy Evening*. He appears to have intended to publish another volume of secular verse in 1647, but did not do so; some of the poems intended for this volume are probably contained in his book *Olor Iscanus*, published in 1651.

By 1646 the Puritan regime had been established in South Wales, and life for Royalist families became hard, for they were fined, heavily taxed, and subjected to numerous indignities. These difficulties, together with the misfortunes of the Church, the death (in July 1648) of a beloved younger brother, and an illness of his own, no doubt contributed to bringing about in Vaughan a greater sobriety and seriousness of mind which culminated in what he himself thought of as a religious conversion. In 1650, the first edition of *Silex Scintillans: or Sacred Poems and Private Ejaculations* appeared. It is in the preface to the second edition of this volume (1655) that Vaughan, after dissociating himself from the poets whom, in his earlier, secular verse, he had imitated ('those ingenious persons, which in the late notion are termed *Wits*'), himself attributes his turning away from secular themes to the influence of 'the blessed man, Mr. *George Herbert*, whose holy *life* and *verse* gained many pious Converts, (of whom I am the least)'. Herbert's influence on Vaughan's poetry will be dealt with in my discussion of the latter.

During the 1650's Vaughan also published a number of prose works, which included two translations of treatises concerned with Hermetic doctrine in its medical aspects. These had perhaps some connection with the fact that Vaughan started to practise as a doctor. We do not know when he took up medicine, but in 1673 he told Aubrey, 'My profession allso is physic, wch I have practised now for many years with good successe (I thank god!) & a repute big enough for a person of greater parts than my selfe.' Where and when Vaughan obtained his professional qualifications, if any, is not known; the addition of 'M.D.' to his name occurs consistently from 1677 onwards, but the title may have been complimentary. However this may be, his practice was large and his patients included such people as the wife of the Bishop of St. Davids.

His wife Catherine, who had borne him four children, died in or about 1653. He married her sister Elizabeth about 1655, and this marriage also resulted in four children. During the remainder of his life he was involved in a number of lawsuits, two of which arose out of disputes with children of the first marriage. The result of one such dispute was that in 1689 his eldest son took over the tenure of Newton, and Vaughan and his wife moved into a cottage at Scethrog. There he spent the rest of his days, continuing to practise medicine to within eighteen months of his death, which occurred on 23rd April 1695. His gravestone is still to be seen in Llansantffraed Churchyard.

POETRY

Vaughan's earlier, secular verse is represented in this selection only by *To Amoret gone from him*, for it is much inferior to the religious poems of *Silex Scintillans*. It is extremely derivative; but what is more important is that the poems seem to be written rather because Vaughan wanted to write poetry than because he has anything urgent to say. When he models himself on Donne, his use of the Metaphysical style suggests the play of fancy rather than the exploration of experience. The poems lack unity, for the author seems more interested in the images themselves than in the themes they are meant to illustrate. Two characteristics of the imagery, however, point forward to the sacred poems: the individual images are often perceptive and striking, and they are often drawn from nature.

The poems of *Silex Scintillans* show that a great development had taken place. The influence of George Herbert, which Vaughan acknowledged, is obvious enough in the abundant borrowings of themes, titles, metrical forms and phrases from *The Temple*. But what Vaughan borrowed he made his own; he did not merely copy. Probably the most important aspect of Herbert's influence was that under it Vaughan experienced feelings and ideals which demanded expression. He had always had talent and perceptiveness, and now he had something to say. He had become interested in the relationship between God and man, as Herbert was; but his interest took forms peculiar to himself. In many poems he contrasts the inconstancy of man towards God with the constancy of natural creation. Other seventeenth-century poets, such as Marvell and Milton, delighted in nature and celebrated its beauties; but Vaughan goes beyond this. Like Wordsworth later, Vaughan looks upon nature as expressing the mind and will of God. Thus the imagery of nature which in his earlier poems had been largely ornamental becomes, in his sacred poems, the means of expressing a living, central experience: a means by which the thought is illustrated, developed and communicated. In these poems, in fact, Vaughan's new-found seriousness of purpose makes him a true Metaphysical poet, handling imagery, diction and movement in the authentic Metaphysical way. It is important, when comparing him with Wordsworth, to remember that though his attitude to nature (and also to childhood: see my note on *The Retreate*) is similar to the latter's, his poetic mode is quite different.

Important as Herbert's influence on Vaughan was, the differences between their work are greater than the similarities. Like Herbert, Vaughan relates spiritual matters to commonplace objects and experiences; but he draws far more on the sights and sounds of nature than Herbert does. He lacks Herbert's economy and perfection of form, so that his poems tend to go on too long and to be memorable in parts rather than as wholes. He has neither the psychological subtlety nor the dramatic sense of Herbert. On the other hand, he can convey ecstatic intensity of feeling; he has a greater gift for the compelling, vivid phrase than Herbert; and his imagery, particularly that of light, has great suggestive power. No one who has once read such lines as:

> I saw Eternity the other night
> Like a great Ring of pure and endless light,

is likely to forget them.

Notes on the Poems of Henry Vaughan

71. TO AMORET GONE FROM HIM

This poem is from *Poems*, 1646. It is characteristic of Vaughan's earlier work in that the conventional 'lover's complaint' theme seems less important than the imagery of nature for which it provides the occasion.

*l.*20. *influence:* an astrological term, referring to an ethereal fluid that was supposed to flow from the heavenly bodies.

*ll.*21–22. An echo of the fourth stanza of Donne's *A Valediction: forbidding mourning.*

72. REGENERATION

This poem and the remainder of the selection from Vaughan are taken from *Silex Scintillans.*

As Sir Herbert Grierson observes, this poem is 'a symbolic parable on the theme: "The wind bloweth where it listeth, and thou hearest the voice thereof, but knowest not whence it cometh, and whither it goeth; so is every one that is born of the Spirit." ' It is particularly notable for its natural description.

*l.*17.   The sense is clear if one imagines a full stop after *still*. The reader will find other places where Vaughan's punctuation is inadequate or misleading.

*l.*25.   *some:* some mysterious voice.

*l.*26.   *led:* having been led.

*l.*28.   *Jacobs Bed: v.* Gen. xxviii. 11–22.

*ll.*63–64.   My restless eye, which was still (or, perhaps, always) searching, espied another object just as strange.

*l.*83.   For v and 17 read iv and 16.

75.   THE RETREATE

This is one of Vaughan's finest poems. It has an economy which much of his work lacks, and its Metaphysical wit and vivid imagery recall Donne.

Like Wordsworth, Vaughan regarded childhood as a time when the soul was closer to God: the child, like the things of nature, is still in harmony with the mind that governs all things. Observe Vaughan's characteristic use of images of light and whiteness to symbolize holiness and purity. The similarity between this poem and Wordsworth's *Intimations of Immortality* has often been commented on.

*l.*4.   *my second race:* in *The Mount of Olives*, Vaughan talks of comparing 'my appointed time here [i.e. in this world] with the portion preceding it, and the eternity to follow'. So the first *race* would be his existence before being born into this world.

76.   THE MORNING-WATCH

This lovely poem exemplifies the ecstatic, singing quality of some of Vaughan's work. The phrase 'Prayer is/The world in tune' (*ll.*18–19) recalls a line from Herbert's *Prayer*—'A kind of tune, which all things heare and fear' and perhaps this was the genesis of Vaughan's poem; but what has developed from it is peculiarly Vaughan's own and essentially different from Herbert's poetry.

*l.*15.   *in their kinds:* in their own ways, according to their natures or species.

77.   PEACE

*ll.*3–4.   *a winged sentrie*, etc.: presumably the Archangel Michael (*v.* Rev. xii. 7).

*l.*17.   *ranges:* this, I think, means 'wanderings'.

*l.*18.   *secure:* make secure, or safe.

78. AND DO THEY SO?

Heading (*Etenim* etc.). Vaughan is quoting the *Codex Bezae*. The Authorized Version gives: 'For the earnest expectation of the creature waiteth for the manifestation of the sons of God.'

l.2.   Influence: see note on *To Amoret gone from him, l.*20. He means 'can they feel more than the "influence" of celestial bodies?'

*ll.*11–16.   Compare Herbert's *Employment, ll.*21–25.

*l.*33.   *abuse:* by disregarding them in favour of *fancies, friends,* or *newes.*

79.   CORRUPTION

Observe the characteristic use of light as a symbol of holiness and nearness to God.

*l.*1.   *those early days:* after the Fall.

*l.*25.   *lay Leiger here:* were resident here.

*l.*40.   See Rev. xiv. 14–15.

81.   THE WORLD

*l.*5.   *the spheres:* see note on Donne's *The Sunne Rising, l.*30.

*l.*16.   *States-man:* statesman, politician.

*ll.*23–24.   The secretive and cunning politician, with his devious methods, is compared to a mole.

*l.*31.   *rust:* See Matth. vi. 19–21.

*l.*34.   *Yet would not place one peece above:* he would not 'lay up' even one piece of treasure in Heaven.

*l.*38.   *plac'd heav'n in sense:* regarded the satisfaction of his senses as Heaven.

*ll.*44–45.   Vaughan has in mind a line from Herbert's *The Church Militant:* 'While Truth sat by, counting his victories'. Here Vaughan envisages Truth as being forced to count not his own victories, but those of the temptations that draw men away from truth.

*ll.*59–60.   In another poem (not in this selection) Vaughan writes of 'that joy . . . which wears heaven like a bridal ring'.

83.   MAN

In this poem, Vaughan contrasts the restlessness of man with the obedience to the Divine will shown by birds, bees and flowers.

*l.*9.   *staidness:* steadiness, constancy.

*l.*10.   *his:* God's.

*l.*15.   *still:* always.

       toyes: trifling amusements.

*l.*23.   *some stones:* loadstones.

84. THEY ARE ALL GONE INTO THE WORLD OF LIGHT!

l.1. They: the dead. Vaughan goes on to liken them to stars.

l.23. what fair Well: Vaughan means 'in the neighbourhood of what fair Well'.

ll.35–36. Vaughan calls upon God to release his soul from this life—*this world of thrall.* Only in Heaven will he find *true liberty.* See Rom. viii. 21.

l.38. perspective: telescope (the first syllable is stressed).

l.40. glass: telescope.

86. THE NIGHT

In John iii. 2 Nicodemus 'came to Jesus by night, and said unto him, Rabbi, we know that thou art a teacher come from God: for no man can do these miracles that thou doest, except God be with him.'

ll.7–12. 'But unto you that fear my name shall the Sun of righteousness arise with healing in his wings . . .' (Malachi iv. 2).

ll.21–22. my Lord is the direct object of *hold* and *lodge.* Vaughan has in mind Luke xxi. 37: 'And every night he went out, and lodged in the mount that is called the mount of Olives.'

l.30. 'And in the morning, rising up a great while before day, he went out, and departed into a solitary place, and there prayed.' (Mark i. 35).

ll.32–35. 'It is the voice of my beloved that knocketh, saying, Open to me, my sister, my love, my dove, my undefiled: for my head is filled with dew, and my locks with the drops of the night.' (Song of Sol. v. 2). See also Rev. iii. 20.

l.39. but: except.

l.42. keep: remain, lodge.

88. QUICKNESS

l.5. Moon-like toil: the moon's toil is to make the tides rise and fall. Vaughan's point is that the moon toils unknowingly and without purpose.

HENRY KING

LIFE

Henry King was born in 1592 at Worminghall, Bucks. He was educated at Westminster School and Christ Church, Oxford. His father, John King, was dean of Christ Church at the time of Henry's matriculation in 1609, and became Bishop of London in 1611, the year in which Henry took his B.A. Soon after this, Henry entered holy orders, and received rapid preferment, becoming Prebend of St. Paul's in 1616 and Archdeacon of Colchester in 1617.

In the same year he married. His wife, whose death in 1624 occasioned his finest poem, *The Exequy*, was Anne Berkeley, of Throwley in Kent. She bore him six children, of whom only two survived infancy. He almost certainly married again in 1630, but the second union produced no children.

In 1639 King became Dean of Rochester; and in 1642, shortly before the outbreak of the Civil War, Bishop of Chichester. He was ejected by the Parliamentary authorities in 1643, and his estates were sequestrated. At the Restoration he recovered his see, and remained there until his death nine years later. He was buried in Chichester Cathedral on 8th October 1669.

His poems were printed anonymously and without his consent in 1657. The only modern edition is a limited one by Mr. J. Sparrow (Nonesuch Press, 1925).

POETRY

Henry King was acquainted with most of the important writers of his time, and was a friend of both Donne and Jonson (he became Donne's executor). These two are clearly the main influences on his poetry, his imagery and wit deriving from the former, and his grace and poise from the latter. His use of language is noteworthy for its fluency and elegance, and in this respect he points forward to the poetry of Pope.

Much of his work is trivial or merely charming, but when inspired by deep feeling he is capable of rising far above his usual level. *The Exequy* is the work of a minor poet, but it seems to me indubitably a major poem, and surely one of the most moving elegies in English. Such lines as these from *The Surrender*:

> We that did nothing study but the way
> To love each other, with which thoughts the day
> Rose with delight to us, and with them set . . .

combine grace with power, and are remarkable for the memorable simplicity of their diction.

Indeed, King's work at its best shows clearly the strength of the Metaphysical mode in which he wrote; his moments of inspiration were comparatively rare, but when they came he was admirably equipped to express them.

89. THE SURRENDER

The occasion of this poem is not known. The theme of parting is not an uncommon one (and indeed this poem reminds one of Michael Drayton's beautiful sonnet, 'Since there's no help, come let us kiss and part'), but it conveys real and moving feeling. It has about it a sort of tender grace which we find also in *The Exequy*, and exemplifies, I think, King's peculiar combination of Metaphysical imagery, language of notable simplicity and economy, and an extraordinary skill in varying the movement of the couplet, particularly by enjambement. Such lines as

> '. . . the rich affections store
> That fed our hopes, lies now exhaust and spent'

have a quality that reminds me of Shakespeare's sonnets.

*ll.*1–2. The punctuation here is somewhat confusing. The sense becomes clear if one realizes that *My once dear Love* is an apostrophe, followed by a parenthesis, *hapless . . . thee so.*

*l.*19. *Cross:* adverse.
envie: envy.

*l.*29. *take home:* take back.

*l.*31. *dislodged:* a trisyllable.

90. THE EXEQUY

This was occasioned by the death of King's first wife, Anne, in 1624. I have already drawn attention in the general Introduction to the speech quality that King introduces into the octosyllabic couplet. Note also how King is able to sustain a sentence over several couplets, as, for example, in the fifth stanza, so that he achieves an effect of flowing continuity and yet uses to the full the controlling and emphasizing effect of the rhymes. T. S. Eliot observes (in his essay 'The Metaphysical Poets' in *Selected Essays*) that the figure of a journey used in lines 89–114 affords a perfect example of the extended comparison, in which 'the idea and the simile become one'.

*l.*11. *blind:* with weeping.

*l.*36. *the earth:* a pun: the shadow of the earth causes an eclipse; earth covers her body, since she is in her grave.

*l.*78. *Monument:* her body, which her soul inhabited and which remains as her 'shrine'.

*l.*101. His vessel steers *from the* Sun in the sense that it steers towards his *West*, i.e. death. This idea is repeated in the image in *l.*102.

*l.*106. *Van:* vanguard of an army.

*ll.*111–112. Notice how the sound of these lines gives the effect of a muffled drum, as at a funeral procession.

94. A CONTEMPLATION UPON FLOWERS

This poem is found in only one MS, where it is signed 'H. Kinge'. Some authorities think it is not his work. Whoever wrote it, it has a quality that reminds one of George Herbert, particularly in the alternation of longer and shorter lines.

ANDREW MARVELL

LIFE

Andrew Marvell was born at Winestead in Holderness, near Hull, on 31st March 1621. His father, an Anglican clergyman, became in 1624 'Lecturer' of Holy Trinity Church, Hull, and Master of the Charterhouse.

Marvell was educated at Hull Grammar School and Trinity College, Cambridge. He left Cambridge in 1640, without taking his M.A., and spent four years travelling on the Continent, during which time he became proficient in several languages.

He took no part in the Civil War, and we cannot be sure which side he favoured, but his poem to Lovelace and his elegy on Lord Hastings suggest that up to 1649 his sympathies were Royalist. His *Horatian Ode upon Cromwel's Return from Ireland*, however, seems to show that by 1650 he had become a moderate supporter of the Parliamentarians. Moreover, early in 1651 we find him installed at Nunappleton House in Yorkshire, as tutor to the daughter of Lord Fairfax. Fairfax had been the leading general of the Parliamentary forces, but had resigned because he opposed Cromwell's aggressive attitude towards the Scots. He had also opposed the execution of Charles I, and was a generous and moderate man, such as Marvell, one imagines, would admire.

Presumably, during his sojourn in the peaceful retirement of Nunappleton, Marvell became convinced that Parliamentary government was in his country's best interests, for in early 1653 he was attempting to enter the government service, as we know from a letter from John Milton to the President of the Council of State, recommending Marvell for employment as an Assistant Latin Secretary. Marvell failed to obtain the appointment at this time, and became instead tutor to Cromwell's ward, William Dutton, in the household of John Oxenbridge at Eton. On 2nd September

1657, however, he was appointed to the Secretaryship for which he had applied in 1653.

After Cromwell's death in 1658, Marvell entered active political life. In 1659 he was elected one of the two Members of Parliament for Hull, which he represented until his death in 1678.

Despite his services to the Commonwealth, Marvell was not only not punished at the Restoration, but was even sent on diplomatic missions to Holland, Russia, Sweden and Denmark. However, he became increasingly opposed to the policies of Charles II, and came into official disfavour because of his criticism of them expressed in his speeches in the Commons and also in his prose and verse satires. The latter were published anonymously; but their authorship was generally known or suspected, and in the last few years of his life Marvell became famous as a pamphleteer.

He died on 16th August 1678, probably of a fever, and was buried in St. Giles in the Fields, London. Most of the work for which he is now famous was not published until after his death, an edition of *Miscellaneous Poems* appearing in 1681. Consequently, it is difficult to assign dates to the individual poems.

So much for the biographical facts: what of the man? To some extent, his character is paradoxical. He was a supporter of the Puritan cause, but there was nothing of the narrow-minded killjoy about him. Indeed, certain opponents criticised him for being a Puritan, yet a frequenter of coffee-houses and a town wit; and, while accusing him of being in the pay of Dissenters, sneered at his fashionable manners, his use of French phrases, and his modish full-bottomed wig. The only real sketch of him by a contemporary is provided by John Aubrey, who writes in *Brief Lives*: 'He was a great master of the Latin tongue; an excellent poet in Latin or English: for Latin verses there was no man could come into competition with him. . . . He was of a middling stature, pretty strong sett, roundish faced, cherry-cheek't, hazell eie, browne haire. He was in his conversation very modest, and of very few words; and though he loved wine he would never drink harde in company, and was wont to say that, *he would not play the good-fellow in any man's company in whose hands he would not trust his life.* He kept bottles of wine at his lodgeing, and many times he would drinke liberally by himselfe to refresh his spirit and exalt his muse.' This account corresponds with the impression one receives from the poems—of liveliness tempered by reserve and conscious control. Aubrey further remarks of him that 'he had not a general acquaintance', and he seems to have chosen his friends with care. They included John Milton and Richard Lovelace, John Pell, the mathematical scholar, James Harrington, the political philosopher, and other men of intellectual distinction.

Yet there was another aspect of his character. He was hot-tempered, and was several times involved in quarrels that came to blows. One of these occurred in the Commons, and when the Speaker called him to order he replied that '. . . the Speaker cast a severe reflection upon him yesterday when he was out of the House: and he hopes that, as the Speaker keep us in order, he will keep himself in order for the future.' His speech when he was roused seems to have been picturesquely forcible; and, though his poems are remarkable for their elegance and urbanity, his satires contain, along with subtle irony, robust and even obscene abuse of his opponents.

Not only his loyalty but his courage is attested by his defence of Milton from persecution in 1660. His pamphleteering, though done anonymously, involved considerable risk; and it seems characteristic that the only time he published a satire under his own name (the second part of *The Rehearsal Transprosed*) he did so in defiance of threats against his life.

His conduct in and attitude towards public affairs seem to have been admirable. His despatches to his constituency show that he represented it conscientiously and painstakingly, and the town of Hull voted funds for a tombstone when he died. As regards the larger issues of the time, he acted with, and fought for, tolerance and sanity. He deplored the violence of the Civil War ('I think the Cause was too good to have been fought for'), but seems to have admired Cromwell as the man best fitted to lead the country in the circumstances of the time. He accepted the Restoration, and upheld the restored monarchy; but there was nothing of the Vicar of Bray about him. His principle seems to have been to make the best of the currently existing form of government, to support what seemed to conduce to the welfare of the country, to strive for sanctity of conscience, and to oppose bigotry and corruption. He criticised Charles II and the Court, while upholding the institution of monarchy. He attacked individual clerics, but not the Church itself. He stood for integrity, and his standards were not partisan but moral.

The character that emerges, then, is that of a man who combined wide culture and subtle wit with moral seriousness; who, though hot-tempered and a redoubtable fighter (as his pamphlets show), was sane and judicious over important issues; and in whom were united, in fact, the best qualities of the Cavalier and the Puritan.

In this selection we are not concerned with Marvell's polemical work; his reputation as a poet depends not upon that, but upon a comparatively few lyrical poems of remarkable quality.

Marvell was not a great poetic originator such as Donne, or even technically inventive as Herbert was, though his handling of verse is masterly. Rather, his work reveals the successful assimilation and fusion of the two great poetic influences of the early seventeenth century: it combines the passionate, probing intellectuality of Donne with the clarity and poise of Jonson. It corresponds largely to the account of Metaphysical Poetry given in the General Introduction to this book; but certain characteristics are particularly noticeable.

In the nineteenth century Marvell was admired for his delight in nature and his skill in natural description, and with good reason. Such lines as these from *The Garden*:

> What wond'rous Life in this I lead!
> Ripe Apples drop about my head;
> The Luscious Clusters of the Vine
> Upon my Mouth do crush their Wine . . .

convey a sensuous delight which reminds us of Keats (particularly the phrase 'luscious clusters'), and which emphasizes that Marvell's Puritanism involved not a gloomy asceticism but a wholesome enjoyment of natural pleasures which he saw as evidence of God's bounty.

But Marvell is now admired for other characteristics as well—characteristics that Mr. T. S. Eliot had in mind when he wrote that the special quality of Marvell's verse is 'a quality of a civilization, of a traditional habit of life'. [1]

The most immediately obvious of these is Marvell's handling of verse. His skill is such that he is able to combine the idiomatic speech-quality of Donne with an elegant polish, a balanced ease, which point forward to Pope. This technical assurance, however, is not mere facility: it expresses a remarkable urbanity of tone—a sense of assured critical detachment which has nothing to do with complacency, but is based on firmly held values. Marvell is assured in manner because his spiritual and cultural standards are sure.

It must be emphasized that Marvell's poise does not involve shallowness of feeling. His best work expresses intense emotion, but the emotion is

[1] 'Andrew Marvell' in *Selected Essays*, Faber & Faber.

controlled, critically explored, and objectified. One of Marvell's leading
characteristics is moral seriousness, but for him seriousness does not mean
single-minded solemnity. He can express serious ideas in witty and
ironical terms, and, conversely, relate an apparently trivial theme or idea
to profoundly important issues. This point needs extended illustration
beyond the scope of this note, but *The Picture of Little T. C. in a Prospect
of Flowers* provides a simple example. The tone of the poem is playful
throughout, but from the last two lines of the third stanza—

> Let me be laid,
> Where I may see thy Glories from some shade—

the sensitive reader realizes that an awareness of mortality underlies the
banter. The little girl becomes identified with the frail and short-lived
flowers, and the injunction to

> Gather the Flow'rs, but spare the Buds;
> Lest *Flora* angry at thy crime,
> To kill her Infants in their prime,
> Do quickly make th' Example Yours . . .

evokes, though still light in tone, a sense of foreboding and of the
poignant possibilities of Nature's power.

Mr. Eliot has defined this aspect of Marvell as 'a recognition, implicit
in the expression of every experience, of other kinds of experience which
are possible.' This recognition is the basis of Metaphysical wit, and is
especially noticeable in Marvell's handling of the conceit and, more
particularly, the pun. For example, in *A Dialogue between the Resolved
Soul, and Created Pleasure*, the Soul, when tempted with the delights of
music, replies,

> Had I but any time to lose,
> On this I would it all dispose.
> Cease Tempter. None can chain a mind
> Whom this sweet Chordage cannot bind.

In this passage, the pun on 'chordage' takes up the idea of bonds first
suggested by 'chain'. Cords are normally thought of as weaker than
chains; yet the suggestion, paradoxically, is that the delicate delights of
music are stronger than any other means which might bind the soul,
their strength lying not in weight or inflexibility but in beauty. 'Sweet
Chordage', moreover, evokes a concrete image of the beauty of music,
and makes us realize that the Soul's reply is no Puritanical condemnation:

music is put aside for a higher aim, with due recognition of its power; and, indeed, is used as a criterion—'if one can prefer the joys of religion to those of music, how wonderful must the former be!' is the implication.

The flexibility of mind and expression that this blend of wit and seriousness represents calls for a corresponding flexibility of response in the reader. Marvell's poetry can be enjoyed for its charm even when read superficially; but the effort to respond fully and alertly to it brings deeper enjoyment still.

NOTES ON THE POEMS OF ANDREW MARVELL

95. A DIALOGUE BETWEEN THE RESOLVED SOUL, AND CREATED PLEASURE

This poem is a debate between two opposed forces. Pleasure speaks in trochaic tetrameter, the Soul in iambic tetrameter. Although the poem is deeply felt and serious, the tone is ironical and there are many puns and double-meanings. The Soul's replies have an epigrammatic quality. The temptations offered by Pleasure deal in turn with the gratification of the five senses and then with the enticements of sex, wealth, glory and knowledge.

l.39. Which refers to the antecedent *Aires*, and is the subject of *recall* and *suspend.*

ll.46–47. fence The Batteries: fence may have a connection with sword-fighting, as some critics suggest; but more probably it means to fight off or ward off, in a general sense. *Batteries* means onslaughts, but carries with it, in opposition to *single*, the suggestion of massed forces such as artillery.

ll.61–62. Gold has no value in itself: it is valued only for its purchasing power; and what it can buy is not worth having.

l.71. Centre: the centre of the earth (and consequently, in Ptolemaic astronomy, of the universe).

l.74. but Humility: but by the degree of Humility.

99. ON A DROP OF DEW

This poem is not only beautiful, but an example of subtle argument carried on by means of the Metaphysical conceit.

ll.5–6. Because it encloses within itself the clear region (Heaven, the region of light) in which it was born.

l.8. native element: heaven.

l.14. the Sphear: the sky (in Ptolemaic astronomy).

l.24. recollecting: collecting again.

l.29. Thus excluding, or shutting out, the world on every side.

ll.37–40. See Exodus xvi. 13–21.

Cromwell had sent a fleet to the Bermudas in 1651 to convert the colony to the Puritan cause. John Oxenbridge, to whose household Marvell went in 1653 as tutor to William Dutton, had twice visited the islands.

Characteristically, the poem expresses both sensuous delight and joyous reverence for Divine benevolence. Observe how Marvell's handling of the octosyllabic couplet suggests the rhythm of the rowing which the song is said to accompany.

l.7. The islands were discovered in 1515 by Juan Bermudez.

l.9. wracks: wrecks, strands.

l.20. Ormus: Ormuz or Hormuz, an ancient town at the mouth of the Persian Gulf. It was an important centre of commerce in the Middle Ages. Milton, like Marvell here, associates it with great wealth (*Par. Lost,* II, 2). *ll.23–24.* Refers to pineapples, introduced by the colonists. These had to be replanted every year.

101. THE NYMPH COMPLAINING FOR THE DEATH OF HER FAUN

It has been suggested that this lovely poem is allegorical, one theory being that it concerns the love of the Church for Christ (the fawn being identified with the Agnus Dei). Certainly the poem contains echoes of the *Song of Solomon,* and great stress is laid on the whiteness of the fawn. Such theories, however, seem to me strained, though they have been ingeniously argued. The echoes of the *Song of Songs* are no more remarkable than other Biblical echoes in the work of other writers, and do not require a mystical explanation. The stress on whiteness—the traditional colour of innocence and purity—is perfectly explicable in terms of the overt theme of the poem, which is about innocence: the Nymph, concerned with her own innocence and the faithlessness of her lover, associates the white fawn with pure love and with the chastity to which she now vows herself. She proposes to fill a vial with the fawn's tears and her own and dedicate them to Diana, the virgin goddess.

The characterization of the Nymph, a simple, Puritan country girl, is charming; and the subtle ambivalence of the poem lies in the reader's awareness of two points of view—the Nymph's and the poet's. Marvell's poise enables him to present both of these without falling into sentimentality on the one hand or cynicism on the other.

ll.3–4. They cannot . . . to kill thee: they could not profit by killing thee.

l.13. It cannot dye so: its death will not be forgotten by Heaven, as she has prayed it should be.

l.17. Deodands: a deodand was a personal possession (it could be a beast or an inanimate object) which, having caused the death of a human being, was forfeited to the Crown as an expiatory offering, to be sold for some pious use. The purpose was to placate the wrath of God ('Deo dandum' means 'to be given to God'). Of course, the deodand, by its nature, was not a reasonable being, and so caused the death without reason or purpose. The point here is that men who kill animals without good reason become degraded to the position of deodands in relation to their victims—become lower than animals, in fact—and will themselves be forfeit to God's anger.

l.53. *then:* than.

l.70. *four:* a disyllable.

l.99. *The brotherless Heliades:* the daughters of the sun. When their brother, Phaethon, was struck down by Zeus, they mourned him until they were turned into poplar trees dropping tears of amber.

l.107. *Elizium:* Elysium, the equivalent, in Greek mythology, of Paradise.

105. TO HIS COY MISTRESS

One of the most famous, and perhaps the greatest, of Marvell's poems. The theme is the familiar and age-old one of 'carpe diem' (enjoy the day, seize the present opportunity), but Marvell's treatment gives it renewed life. The poem also shows us how much of the Cavalier there was about Marvell, despite his Puritan affiliations. We do not know, however, whether it was addressed to a real person and seriously intended.

Note the logical development (if . . . but . . . therefore); the combination of wit and intensity of feeling; the dramatic change of tone after the first paragraph; and the passionate conviction of the close. T. S. Eliot's essay, already mentioned, contains a brilliant analysis of this poem.

l.10. The conversion of the Jews, according to ancient tradition, would occur immediately before the end of the world.

l.34. *dew:* the 1681 folio gives *glew*, but this is probably the printer's error in repeating the *g* of *morning.* Some editors read *dew*; others *lew*, meaning warmth.

l.40. *slow-chapt pow'r: chapt* refers to jaws (chaps or chops). The meaning is that time would slowly devour them.

107. THE DEFINITION OF LOVE

Whereas *To his Coy Mistress* urged the fulfilment of desire, this poem despairs at its impossibility. The influence of Donne is more marked than in any other of Marvell's poems. Note the geometrical and astronomical images, and the frequent use of paradox.

l.20. *by themselves:* by each other.

l.24. *Planisphere:* a plane projection of the Globe.

ll.31-32. Marvell is playing upon *Conjunction* and *Opposition* as astronomical terms. In astronomy, *Conjunction* refers to the state of being in

apparent union of heavenly bodies, while *Opposition* means the situation of
two heavenly bodies when their longitudes differ by 180°.

109. Lines from UPON APPLETON HOUSE—THE GARDEN

Upon Appleton House is a poem of ninety-seven stanzas, far too long for
inclusion in this volume. These famous lines, describing Lord Fairfax's
garden, are taken from Stanzas XXXIX–XLII. They are noteworthy not
only for the ingenious conceit of describing the garden in military terms,
but also for the patriotism and the sorrow for the ravages of the Civil War
that they express.

l.12.   or: probably means 'nor', i.e. without asking.

l.15.   four: a disyllable.

110.   THE PICTURE OF LITTLE T. C. IN A PROSPECT OF FLOWERS

Little T. C. may have been Theophila Cornewall. She was baptized in
1644; so, assuming she was about eight years old when the poem was
written, it can be dated 1652.

l.12.   Love: Cupid.

l.22.   but: only.

l.36.   Flora: Roman goddess of flowers and gardens.

111.   THE GARDEN

This great poem has been the subject of much commentary and discussion.
The garden described so sensuously is presumably that at Nunappleton
House. It is used as a symbol of innocence and peace, and compared with the
Garden of Eden—before the creation of Eve.

l.2.   Palm: a palm branch or leaf was a symbol of victory.

   Oke: an oak garland was bestowed as the civic crown.

   Bayes: a garland of bay-laurel, awarded as an honour to poets.

l.17.   White and red: colours emblematic of female beauty.

ll.29–30.   Apollo sought to force his love on Daphne, a mountain nymph
and celibate priestess of Mother Earth. She fled from him in vain, but
Mother Earth saved her from his embrace by turning her into a laurel-tree.

ll.31–32.   The nymph Syrinx similarly fled from the god Pan and, on her
prayer for rescue, was turned into a reed.

l.37.   curious: exquisite.

l.41.   from pleasure less: the meaning of this is uncertain. William Empson
suggests (in his essay on the poem in *Determinations,* ed. F. R. Leavis) two
possibilities, both of which I find completely unconvincing. I consider that
the most probable meaning is arrived at if we understand the phrase as *from
pleasure which is less.* Thus Marvell means that the mind withdraws from the

lesser (because physical) pleasures described in the previous stanza, into the bliss of detached contemplation.

ll.43–44. Refers to the belief discussed by Sir Thomas Browne (*Pseudodoxia Epidemica*, III, xxiv) 'That all Animals of the land are in their kind in the Sea'.

ll.47–48. Prof. Margoliouth points out that these lines are ambiguous: 'They may mean either "reducing the whole world to nothing material, i.e. to a green thought", or "considering the whole material world as of no value compared to a green thought".' He considers that the second interpretation harmonizes better with *transcending these*. *A green thought:* self-contemplation in complete detachment from the world; a state of impersonal contemplation.

l.54. whets: preens.

ll.65–66. The reference is to a floral sundial.

114. AN HORATIAN ODE UPON CROMWEL'S RETURN FROM IRELAND

This poem was cancelled from all known copies of the 1681 folio but two and was not republished until 1776. The cancellation was presumably for political reasons.

Cromwell returned from Ireland in May 1650. As the poem deals with his return and looks forward to the Scottish campaign, which began in July, it was presumably written during the early summer of 1650.

The poem is remarkable for its political and religious objectivity. Marvell pays tribute to Charles I's courage and majesty on the scaffold, but realizes the inevitability of his execution. He speaks of Cromwell as of a man ordained by Destiny to bring about the creation of a new order: a man without personal ambition, and almost like a force of nature himself.

The poem has the grandeur of a Horatian Ode. The metre is Marvell's own invention, and remarkably successful in suggesting gravity, vigour and the inexorable march of events.

l.1. The youth who wishes to appear forward (i.e. ready for the requirements of the time).

l.15. Side: the cloud is thought of as the body of the lightning, so the emerging lightning bursts through its own side. Similarly, taking *side* as meaning *party*, Cromwell rose swiftly to eminence from his place among the other Parliamentary leaders.

l.24. Laurels were believed to be proof against lightning.

l.32. Bergamot: a kind of pear. It is perhaps significant that it was known as 'the pear of Kings'.

l.42. penetration: this refers to the supposed occupation of the same space by two bodies at the same time. Nature tolerates *penetration* even less than a vacuum, which she abhors.

*ll.*47-52. Charles I fled from Hampton Court to Carisbrooke Castle on the Isle of Wight. Marvell is referring to the theory that Cromwell deliberately frightened Charles into fleeing from Hampton Court for his own ends, since the King's flight was one of the causes of his dethronement and execution.

       case: a pun, the two meanings being 'plight' and 'cage or prison'.

*l.*54. *Scaffold:* another pun, since the word also meant 'stage'.

*l.*60. The Latin *acies* means both eyesight and blade. *Try* means put to the test.

*l.*66. which first confirmed or made safe the power that had been gained by force.

*ll.*67-72. When the foundations of the temple of Jupiter on the summit of the Capitoline hill in Rome were being dug, a human head was discovered, and this was taken as an omen of good fortune for the State.

*l.*74. *one year:* Cromwell landed in Ireland on 15th August 1649.

*l.*104. *Clymacterick:* means critical, bringing about a new epoch.

*l.*106. *party-colour'd:* a play on the derivation of Pict from the Latin *pingere*, to paint or colour, and a jibe at the Scots for the untrustworthiness and treachery which their recent history was considered to demonstrate.

*l.*107. *sad:* (i) steadfast, (ii) dull or dark in colour (in contrast to *party-colour'd*).

*l.*110. *Mistake:* because his plaid would camouflage him, acting as an animal's protective colouring does.

*ll.*117-118. A cross-hilted sword, having the shape of a crucifix, would frighten away evil spirits.

ABRAHAM COWLEY

LIFE

Abraham Cowley was born in Fleet Street, London, in 1618, the posthumous son of a wealthy stationer and bookseller. He was a child prodigy: he wrote an epic romance at the age of ten, and published his first volume of poems, *Poeticall Blossomes*, in his fifteenth year, while still at Westminster School.

In 1637 he went up, as a scholar, to Trinity College, Cambridge. In 1640 he became a Fellow of the college, and in 1641 he wrote a comedy which was acted at Trinity before Prince Charles. While at Cambridge he became the close friend of Richard Crashaw.

In 1643 he was ejected from his fellowship by the Parliamentarians, and went to Oxford, where the Court had established itself. He became cipher-secretary to the Queen, Henrietta Maria, and accompanied her to Paris.

In 1655 he returned to England as a Royalist spy, and was arrested and imprisoned. After a short time, he was released and went to Oxford, where he studied medicine, becoming M.D. in 1657.

At the Restoration, Cowley was restored to his fellowship and received the grant of the manor of Oldcourt from the Queen; but he did not consider that his services to the Royalist cause had been sufficiently rewarded. He retired to the country, to Chertsey. The publication of his volume of love poems, *The Mistress*, in 1647 had gained him a high reputation, which had steadily increased so that during the years of his retirement he was regarded as the leading figure in English letters. Denham compared him to Virgil, Dryden regarded him with veneration, and half a century after his death Samuel Johnson described him as 'undoubtedly the best' of the Metaphysical poets. The significance of these judgments will be seen when we consider his poems.

His last years were spent in studying medicine and botany and writing *Essays in Verse and Prose* (pub. 1668). He was one of the founders of the Royal Society, which received its charter in 1662. He died in 1667.

POETRY

Cowley's great reputation after the Restoration was due to the fact that though he wrote in a Metaphysical manner (actually he wrote in other styles as well, such as that of the Pindaric ode; but we are concerned here only with his Metaphysical poetry) in so far as he used conceits, puns, argument, and so on, his mind was radically different from Donne's. He lacked intensity of passion and depth of insight. His wit is a matter of ingenuity, and his images are usually decorative and fanciful, rather than a means of exploring experience or resolving conflict. He lacks the fusion of thought and feeling which produces the characteristic Metaphysical intensity, and the experiences he conveys are less complex.

In reading Cowley's work one becomes aware of the attitudes and the tone of the Age of Reason (one remembers Cowley's scientific interests): of standards of politeness and decorum, and disciplined common sense. His mind is a Restoration mind, perfectly congenial to such contemporaries as Dryden; and this comes out clearly in such lines as these, from the poem, *Of Wit*:

> All ev'ry where, like *Mans*, must be the *Soul*,
> And *Reason* the *Inferior Powers* controul.

It is, in fact, the Augustan tendency in Cowley which made him so popular in his own time and well into the eighteenth century. He wrote in the Metaphysical manner, and his work could be enjoyed as 'fanciful' or 'quaint', but it made no demands on Augustan readers such as they found uncongenial in Donne. As Sir Herbert Grierson observes,[1] in Cowley 'the central heat [of Metaphysical poetry] has died down. Less extravagant, his wit is also less passionate and imaginative. The long wrestle between reason and the imagination has ended in the victory of reason, good sense . . . the fashion of 'metaphysical' wit remains in Cowley's poems when the spirit that gave it colour and music is gone.'

Notes on the Poems of Abraham Cowley

118. OF WIT

Dr. F. R. Leavis comments (*Revaluation*, p. 30) that in this poem Cowley 'discusses and expounds wit in a manner and spirit quite out of resonance with the Metaphysical mode—quite alien and uncongenial to it; with a reasonableness that has little to do with the "tough reasonableness" underlying Marvell's lyric grace . . . It is a spirit of good sense; appealing to criteria that the coming age will refine into "Reason, Truth and Nature".' Both Cowley's conception of wit and the images by which he presents it show a superficiality far removed from Metaphysical wit.

*l.*12. *Zeuxes Birds:* Zeuxis was a famous Greek painter of 5th century B.C. He was said to be so skilful that birds came to peck at his picture of a bunch of grapes.

*l.*14. *Multiplying Glass:* a lens with a number of facets giving many reflections of an object. This and the following image remind us of Cowley's scientific interests.

*ll.*17–18. 'So it is that the title of "a wit", the highest fame can bestow, is bestowed so often.'

*l.*20. *Tit'lar Bishops:* Cowley refers to the creation in Rome of Roman Catholic bishops of sees in England. As they were excluded from England, their bishoprics were titular only.

*l.*29. *Numbers:* verses.

*ll.*29–30. Amphion played the harp so skilfully that when he and his brother fortified Thebes his music caused stones to move and build themselves into a wall.

*l.*40. ⸱ *the Galaxie:* The Milky Way.

*l.*50. *Bajazet:* Bajazeth, Emperor of the Turks, in Marlowe's *Tamburlaine the Great.*

*l.*52. *short lung'd Seneca:* Seneca, the Roman philosopher and dramatist, noted for his epigrammatic style.

[1] *Metaphysical Poetry, Donne to Butler*, p. lvi.

ll.61–64. The reference is to Plato's 'Theory of Ideas', according to which all actual things are mere imperfect copies of archetypes, or perfect and eternal patterns, which exist outside the world of sense.

120 ON THE DEATH OF MR. CRASHAW

This is Cowley's best Metaphysical poem. However, the style of the poem varies, and several parts of it—the balanced, self-contained nature of the couplets in such sections as the first two paragraphs; the use of the alexandrine; and the grandiose manner of, for example, the last paragraph—have a Restoration quality.

For an account of Crashaw's death and Cowley's friendship with him, see Life of Crashaw, p. 155.

l.17. *Numbers:* poetry, verses.

l.18. *The Heav'nliest thing on Earth:* poetry.

l.20. *Calves at Bethel: v.* 1 Kings xii, 28–33.

l.21. Cowley seems to be uniting two legends here: (*a*) that Pan's death coincided with the birth of Christ; (*b*) that Christ's birth caused all oracles to become mute (cf. Milton: *On the Morning of Christ's Nativity*, st. XIX).

l.22. *the Fiend Apollo:* Apollo was the god of poetry, and his oracles were famous. The point of 'fiend' is that the pagan gods were identified with devils: hence in *Paradise Lost* Milton gives the fallen angels the names of pagan deities.

l.28. *Fabulous:* given to fabling.

l.30. *she:* Crashaw's Muse.

ll.33–34. 'And scorned to take as Mistress any but the Virgin Mary.' Cowley means that Crashaw, instead of writing love poems to a mortal woman, devoted himself to extolling the Virgin.

ll.35–36. Just as the Blessed Virgin bore the Christ-child, so Crashaw's pure Muse brought forth poetry.

ll.37–46. See Life of Crashaw.

ll.47–48. Crashaw had abandoned the Anglican faith, and become a Roman Catholic. Cowley here apologizes for praising an apostate.

l.55. *nice Tenents:* subtle or difficult points of doctrine.

ll.65–66. Elijah was carried up to heaven in a chariot of fire. See 2 Kings iii for this and the references in *ll*.67–72.

ll.67–68. Elisha was the successor as prophet of Elijah. Elisha's 'wish', expressed to Elijah, was 'let a double portion of thy spirit be upon me'. Cowley's wish is more modest, as befits his own *Littleness* in relation to Crashaw's *Greatness*: he asks (*l*.71) not for a 'double portion' but for *Half thy mighty Spirit.*

Cowley wrote this poem near the end of his life. It is an impressive piece, but there is little of the true Metaphysical depth about the images: they are little more than a series of decorative illustrations of the power of light.

ll.2–4.   The grammar is perhaps confusing. *Negro, which, it,* and *the melancholly Mass* all refer to Chaos.

ll.7–8.   A reference to Zeus (Jove) and Danaë. See note on *l.*8 of Carew's *Song: Mediocrity* etc.

l.21.   *Carriere:* career, course.

l.23.   *Post-Angel:* presumably an angel travelling to earth as a messenger.

l.29.   *Scythian-like:* the Scythians were nomadic.

l.44.   *antick:* antic, grotesque.

l.46.   *conscious:* conscious, presumably, of their guilt and obscenity.

l.83.   *Flora:* goddess of flowers.

l.102.   *Empyraean Heaven:* in the old cosmology, the Empyrean was the highest heaven, the sphere of the pure element of fire, and, to Christians, the abode of God.

INDEX OF FIRST LINES